Rugby Union and Globalization

Global Culture and Sport

Series Editors: **Stephen Wagg** and **David Andrews**

Titles include:

John Harris
RUGBY UNION AND GLOBALIZATION
An Odd-Shaped World

Roger Levermore and Aaron Beacom (*editors*)
SPORT AND INTERNATIONAL DEVELOPMENT

Pirkko Markula (*editor*)
OLYMPIC WOMEN AND THE MEDIA
International Perspectives

Global Culture and Sport
Series Standing Order ISBN 978–0–230–57818–0 hardback
978–0–230–57819–7 paperback
(*outside North America only*)

You can receive future titles in this series as they are published by placing a standing order. Please contact your bookseller or, in case of difficulty, write to us at the address below with your name and address, the title of the series and the ISBN quoted above.

Customer Services Department, Macmillan Distribution Ltd, Houndmills, Basingstoke, Hampshire RG21 6XS, England

---

Rugby Union and Globalization

An Odd-Shaped World

John Harris
Kent State University, USA

First published 2010 by
PALGRAVE MACMILLAN

Palgrave Macmillan in the UK is an imprint of Macmillan Publishers Limited, registered in England, company number 785998, of Houndmills, Basingstoke, Hampshire RG21 6XS.

Palgrave Macmillan in the US is a division of St Martin's Press LLC, 175 Fifth Avenue, New York, NY 10010.

Palgrave Macmillan is the global academic imprint of the above companies and has companies and representatives throughout the world.

Palgrave® and Macmillan® are registered trademarks in the United States, the United Kingdom, Europe and other countries.

ISBN 978–0–230–22931–0   hardback

This book is printed on paper suitable for recycling and made from fully managed and sustained forest sources. Logging, pulping and manufacturing processes are expected to conform to the environmental regulations of the country of origin.

A catalogue record for this book is available from the British Library.

A catalog record for this book is available from the Library of Congress.

10   9   8   7   6   5   4   3   2   1
19   18   17   16   15   14   13   12   11   10

Printed and bound in Great Britain by
CPI Antony Rowe, Chippenham and Eastbourne

In memory of
William Derek James
for showing me the way

Contents

Acknowledgements

A number of people have played an important role in this project. My family is always there for me and provides unconditional love and support. Numerous people have offered pointers along the way whether it was just to answer one of my many random questions or to point me in the direction of readings. I am grateful to those in the rugby and academic worlds who have taken time to do this. Steve Wagg and Dave Andrews supported this project from the outset and kindly offered guidance and expertise in framing the focus. At Palgrave Macmillan I thank Philippa Grand and Olivia Middleton for taking this on and Macmillan Publishing Solutions for the efficient and professional copy-editing work. While a mother-in-law is not often acknowledged in texts on sport, mine generously provides sporting literature (and the key writing tools of coffee and chocolate) from over the pond and so deserves a special mention.

Over the years I have enjoyed working with a number of people on research that has nothing to do with rugby but has been valuable in developing my writing and ways of thinking about the social and cultural landscape of sport. My collaborative work with Ben Clayton on a range of sporting celebrities certainly influenced the way in which Chapter 4 has evolved and although I make explicit reference to our work on rugby and metrosexual identity, much of our other research on sporting celebrities, while not directly relevant to the present study, has certainly shaped and informed my analysis in this area.

The great challenges faced when moving nations is an experience shared by many migrant workers including rugby players and coaches. For Danielle and I moving to the US proved a greater challenge and a bigger culture shock than we were ever prepared for. The kindness and warm welcome shown by a number of people made our adjustment possible and it would be remiss of me not to say a big thank you to Sue, Quinn, Theresa, Mark & Julie, Steve & Caroline, Kim, Andy & Josephine and others who helped us adapt to living in a foreign country. A special *diolch yn fawr* must also be made to Brian, Rhonda, Jenna and Logan – our surrogate family in Ohio without whom our US adventure would have been so much shorter.

My biggest debt of gratitude though, goes to my wife, Danielle, who shows remarkable patience and understanding in support of my working on this text when there are always many other things that need to be done. As someone who likes and understands the game she has also kindly read through the work and offered numerous suggestions on drafts of the various chapters. During the course of thinking about and (finally) writing this book life was turned upside down by the birth of our son Thomas Wyn. His early morning wake-up calls, and night-time visits, meant that this book became a true 24/7 project and parts of it were written at hours of the day that I had last seen by the side of a kebab van many years before. He is too young to understand why his Dad keeps disappearing to type a few more words on the computer but he makes every day special and is our world.

Prologue

I was once told that I talked a good game of rugby. As a scrum-half of limited ability there was little chance that Gareth Edwards would lose his position as the greatest number nine in the history of the sport to me. It is hoped that friends and family who have no choice but to read this book will acknowledge that I am indeed a better writer of rugby than I ever was a player. This text is written from the premise that all work is firmly located and needs to be read and understood in a particular time and place. To this end the focus of this book is on rugby union since 1995. Yet although this year marked the beginning of open professionalism in the sport it was not the year zero and I reflect upon the many changes to rugby since this change through reference to the game in the amateur era. Within the following pages I try to analyse rugby's open professionalism within and alongside the process of globalization.

Unlike much of the published work on sport and globalization, I do not follow one particular theoretical approach in developing the arguments put forward in this text. This is not intended as a criticism of such work, for this study draws heavily on much of the valuable groundbreaking work undertaken by scholars aligned to a particular theoretical stance. It is based on the premise that all understanding takes place within a particular social and cultural context so it is important to recognize the situatedness of any work. Globalization is a contested concept and continues to reshape how we study the social world (Robinson, 2007). Globalization is also a ubiquitous concept that continues to (re)shape our everyday lives. Yet it is also important to provide a reflexive account of any analysis involving discussions of globalization for we all see the world from somewhere in particular. As will become apparent in the following pages, this study is shaped by a variety of the works on aspects of globalization. In a broader sense, and relating to my wider work within sport, the sociological imagination espoused by C. Wright Mills and the cultural studies approach of Raymond Williams are clear influences on my understanding. For someone born in Wales but now working in the US, this coupling represents an appropriate point of departure for this work. I am pretty sure that Mills never took to the rugby field in the US but Williams, like all good Welsh schoolboys, played the game at school in Abergavenny. Identifying and recognizing the situated limits of research represents both a strength and weakness of any study, particularly one that aims to examine the relationship between the local and the global.

Reflections of the disinterested sociologist

Born and raised in Wales, where rugby is perceived to be the national sport, my interest and understanding of the game is firmly located and undoubtedly influenced by the positioning of rugby within and around the promotion and celebration of national identity in the Principality. Indeed one of the real challenges for anyone writing about a subject like sport is not to look at certain issues through rose-tinted glasses and fall into a romanticized portrayal of the imagined and invented traditions that shape our social worlds even though sport may be especially susceptible to such positioning for it can be such an emotive issue.

As Smith (2008: p. xiv) perceptively notes, 'sport has a rich conceptual framework' and 'we see what we want to see when we watch sport'. The world of academia dictate that work should be critical and reflexive and attempt to unpack some of our own assumptions and taken-for-granted views. Here to be recognized as a 'scholar' one must submit their works to learned journals where experts can offer critiques of the research. One of the politer critiques of my work, in the dark arena of the anonymous peer-review process, suggested that the writing seemed to be 'more like that of a rugby enthusiast than the disinterested sociologist'. I am still not quite sure what a 'disinterested sociologist' is for the heart of sociological inquiry is guided by the itch to know things. For Mills (1959) it was the interplay of biography and history that shaped sociological thought and that to 'be a good craftsman' a social analyst must try to have a good grasp of the relations between the two. By this it is clear that within any particular space there is a hegemonic ideology or code that shapes it. Yet it is also important to note that while something may be dominant 'it is never either total or exclusive' (Williams, 1977: p. 113). So in trying to accurately portray just where this book is written from, I state clearly that it is reflective of a particular time and a particular place.

As a book about the competing demands of tradition and change, and the relationship between the local and the global, it is also a critical account of the governance of international rugby and the development of the sport.

Many of the ideas were first conceived and developed when working over the border in that country to the East of Wales. When asked where Welsh rugby would now go after a heavy defeat by New Zealand in the first ever world cup competition in 1987, the then Wales Manager Clive Rowlands remarked that it would probably have to be back to beating England every year. Sadly 'Top Cat's' prophecy was remarkably short-lived and much of my early academic career living and working in England was a period where Wales suffered numerous heavy defeats at the hands of the men in white. During this time my esteemed colleagues regularly reminded me of this fact and although I know that much of their abuse may have stemmed from jealousy of not being born on the right side of the border I am pleased to still consider them as friends.

As a visible reflection of globalization, and in particular the significance of transcontinental migration to this inter-connectedness between people and places, the book has been written in the state of Ohio in the US. Here rugby is very much a minority activity and occupies a marginal place in the sporting landscape of the country. Being Welsh, and conforming to national stereotypes, on arriving in the US I was asked to assist with coaching the University's rugby team. This was a fantastic experience and something I enjoyed immensely. Working with this group of players provided a new impetus and encouraged a very different thinking in my understanding of the sport. Teaching in a state university, including a course on sport in a global perspective, further opened my eyes to the ways in which we each make sense of the world and conceive of different people and places. Indeed while I have had the opportunity to visit a number of nations for conferences and the like, it is interesting to consider how this may reflect the life of a professional rugby player and that often we see little beyond the confines of a hotel and conference facility (or hotel, training field and rugby pitch for the latter). To spend an extended period within a different country and learn more about a particular culture is key to really understanding more about aspects of globalization and local/global intersections within different contexts. Living in a different environment also allows you to critically reflect upon your own sense of place, and understanding of identity, in a way that remaining rooted in 'the local' never can. For Mills (1959) this would be best articulated as encompassing semantics (establishing what something is in itself) and syntax (establishing what it is not) in furthering this understanding.

I recall one of our rugby matches being delayed because there were no pads on the base of the posts. I think this was because the women's team had forgotten to return them from the previous week but the referee was adamant that the game could not start until these had been found. Given that the playing surface resembled a recently ploughed field and included what could best be described as a ditch, where our small scrum-half was only visible by his curly mop of hair, the sudden focus on safety seemed rather strange. Indeed, had the referee witnessed our performance the previous week he would have realized that the posts were probably one of the safest places on the pitch! Phone calls were made and a pick-up truck arrived with the remnants of an old sofa, probably trashed at the last party, flapping around in the back. These were then painstakingly taped around the base and the game could finally begin. This is just one example of the many barriers that this group of men had to over-come to play the game they had grown to love. Players like these, across the continents, represent the true heart and soul of the game and a world removed from the environment of psychologists, nota-tional analysts and nutritionists that increasingly characterize the sport at the elite level today.

From Wales to the US represents two extremities in the global rugby landscape, yet it is also important to recognize that they are only separated by ten places in the International Rugby Board world rankings (IRB, 2009). To illustrate the challenges of developing rugby as a truly international game a second/third string Welsh side, minus their leading players touring with the British and Irish Lions, easily beat the strongest US team in 2005 and 2009 thereby highlighting the massive gap between the 'haves' and 'have-nots' of international rugby. In terms of trying to provide insights into the development of rugby union since 1995 and how the forces of commercialism and consumer capitalism have reshaped the game I look at the sport in a range of different contexts but the very dominance of a small group of core nations regarding all aspects of the sport deems that they are part of the story more than others. It attempts to critically examine the relationship between the local and the global in different places. While every attempt is made to provide examples from across different parts of the world the cases used are both deliberately selective and, as a result of my own experiences and linguistic capacities, necessarily limited. Part of the challenge with trying to understand and write about something as complex and contested as globalization is that the very nature of the subject means that it is impossible to touch upon all aspects of global flows even in one particular sport. Rugby's biggest challenge, to develop a truly global presence, lies in its somewhat insular and narrow outlook. This resultant connectivity between a relatively small group of nations dictates that much of the book comments on how rugby has failed to embrace globalization.

Two things I tried to do from the outset was to avoid using endnotes and to keep the language as clear and concise as possible. While I have succeeded in the first goal, the very nature of the subject and the language employed in the established literature means that I have been less successful in the latter. It is hoped that I have managed to get the points across as clearly as possible and have been able to write a better game of rugby than I ever played.

Rugby and globalization: Starting in Bridgend

Routes and roots form a big part of this text; and although the present journey and moving between different places have certainly shaped my thinking about rugby and globalization, it is also firmly rooted in my past. This book was written in the US and owes much to living in England, but its real inceptions can be traced to Bridgend in South Wales. At the Brewery Field in the town Boxing Day derby matches against Maesteg were always a highlight of the festive season. Rumour had it that it was always best if we attacked the brewery end of the ground in the second half as the smell from there would spur the players on. So although growing up on the Gwent border, where most of my classmates' rugby affiliations were to the formidable forward power of Pontypool, I always supported Bridgend.

In Bridgend it was my Uncle Derek who unknowingly provided me with much of the inspiration to pursue a career of reading, writing and talking about sport (aka academia). His collection of sports books were something I relished reading from a very early age and our conversations about rugby at the dining table, as my Aunty Marlyn kept us stocked up on tea and cake, were a big part of this fascination with rugby union and sport in general that has provided me with opportunities to see different places and meet many interesting people. As a proud and long-serving postman in Bridgend, sometime in the early 1990s he worked with a young man named Gareth Thomas whose father was also employed at the same depot. Rugby then was still an amateur sport so its leading players worked in a range of professions and even the biggest stars still had to find ways of paying their mortgage, feeding their families and/or having enough money in the pocket to enjoy the festivities that followed a rugby match. For more than a century rugby was about the postmen, publicans, plasterers and policemen who played the game for no financial gain but solely for the love of the sport.

More than a decade on and 'Alfie' no longer worked at the depot for a successful career in professional rugby encompassing plying his trade for Toulouse in France, captaining both his country and the British and Irish Lions, meant that he was one of the best paid players in the country. Gareth Thomas was one of the last of a group of men for whom playing rugby and its associated aspirations initially stretched as far as 'going out on the piss with the boys' (Thomas, 2007: p. 47) and enjoying the game with their friends. Now boys growing up in Bridgend, Southampton or Columbus can aspire to a career as a rugby player and a life as a full-time professional athlete. Yet despite the great strides forward made in many aspects of the game, and the seismic shifts that have occurred to reshape the sporting landscape today, their options may still be somewhat limited and it is only in a select small number of nations that a man can earn a living solely by playing rugby union.

This text is certainly not the final word on rugby union and globalization. Indeed the work clearly highlights the need for further research on many areas that need to be better understood and that there are pressing issues to be resolved. Moreover, the rapid transformations brought about by open professionalism, intensified globalization and its related impacts mean that the game has changed more in the last 15 years than it did in the 100 years preceding that. The sport continues to alter at a remarkable speed and recent developments such as the proposed addition of Italian teams to the Magners League and the potential addition of Argentina to an expanded Super 15 and Four-Nations competition are reflective of this. Perhaps most significantly the inclusion of Rugby Sevens in the 2016 Olympic Games means that the sport is 'reaching out' in a way not seen before. Yet it is also important not to get carried away by these developments and to try and provide a measured evaluation of the current state of play. Richard Burton once suggested that rugby is a game of massive lies and stupendous exaggerations. Many of the claims made on its apparent globalization would appear to fall into this category for the sport remains dominated by a very select group of nations and a small cohort of men. In the period since 1995 the blazers may have had to accommodate the suits but they continue to keep control of the ball and dictate just how and where the game is played.

JH
Kent, Ohio.

Introduction

Roots and Routes I: A (Very) Brief Overview of Globalization

As outlined in the prologue, roots and routes form a central part in exploring aspects of the relationship between rugby union and globalization. As Hall (1990) has noted, this shows how identity should be seen as belonging as much to the future as it does to the past. This clearly illustrates the quest to move beyond rigid conceptions of identity and also points to how in an increasingly globalized age our identities are more likely to be provisional, contingent and relatively unfixed. In social identities research it is clear that collective identities tend to focus on issues of similarity whereas individual identities focus more on difference. As MacClancy (1996) has noted, sports are embodied practices through which new meanings can be established (see also, Harris and Parker, 2009). Looking at aspects of the local and global in a particular sport presents fertile ground for further examining the connectedness between roots and routes in varied contexts and within the wider discourse of globalization.

Globalization has markedly altered the social and cultural landscape of sport where the ideas and language of business dominates as activities become more than 'just a game' and part of an international entertainment industry (Amis and Cornwell, 2005; Slack, 2004). Sport is no different from various other spheres where markets are carefully managed for maximum profit and labour migration is commonplace. John Williams (1994) noted how traditional notions of connections between sport, community and place seem especially vulnerable in 'the age of satellites global flows' (p. 390). While this comment was written with reference to the sport of association football, it is a particularly pertinent point to apply to rugby union in the period since 1995 when a large media contract from Rupert Murdoch's News Corporation effectively signaled the end of (sh)amateurism in the sport.

Writing more broadly about globalization, Robins (1991) has highlighted the ways in which the compression of time and space horizons has created a world of instantaneity and depthlessness, a decentred space where frontiers and boundaries have become permeable. In this sense it is argued that 'routes' have replaced 'roots' as local rootedness has been superseded by global interconnection (Back, 1998). Yet rugby also remains very much about place, local heroes and pride in the performances of 'our boys' or, as numerous writers have highlighted, the global does not simply replace the local in an all-encompassing, overreaching way (e.g. Appadurai, 1990; Robertson, 1995; Tomlinson, 1999). As Giulianotti (2005) posits we can be neither 'for' nor 'against' globalization. Instead we should recognize that globalization has become 'an ontological dimension of social life, a kind of multi-faceted social fact' (Giulianotti, 2005: p. 190). More realistically then, it is better to acknowledge that the local and the global interact with each other in multifarious ways and it is the interaction between them that forms the underpinning of this work.

Globalization has become one of the most pressing issues for scholars in the social sciences and a range of other associated disciplines where a field of globalization studies continues to emerge across these disciplines (Appelbaum and Robinson, 2005). Numerous academics have written on the subject, addressing the concept of globalization from a wide array of different perspectives (see especially, Albrow, 1996; Beck, 2000; Ritzer, 2007; Robertson, 1992; Scholte, 2000; Tomlinson, 1999; Veseth, 2005). It is beyond the scope of this study to make reference to all of the various positions adopted in this large and ever-expanding field of global studies. Kellner (2002) has noted that the concept of globalization is a theoretical construct that 'varies according to the assumptions and commitments of the theory in question' (p. 301). The discussion and observations I put forward in this work are not aligned to any one particular theoretical stance and instead draws upon ideas and insights from a range of schools of social thought.

Part of the problem with globalization is its seemingly overused employment as a catch-all term of academic writing to mean many things. As Miller et al. (2001) noted, the term has supplanted postmodernity in sociology and cultural studies as an omnibus concept used to explain transformations and describe their outcomes in a totalizing fashion (see also, Rowe, 2003), while Kellner (2002: p. 285) refers to globalization as 'the buzzword of the 1990s'. Having said that there can still be some confusion as to exactly what is meant by globalization with some dominant discourse still largely framing it within a language that is presenting a thesis of Americanization. While there is no denying that the US has a hegemonic status in many spheres of globalization, this is not always the case in sport per se and certainly not in rugby. As Bairner (2001) suggests, in an informed discussion of the perceived Americanization of sport, it is doubtful that much of this reflects Americanization as opposed to 'the evolution of capitalism' (p. 15). Allison's (2005) work is also useful in teasing out some of the key issues here in relation to the sporting world and Veseth's (2005) wider analysis draws out some of the central issues in highlighting the limitations of the Americanization thesis. Veseth (2005) highlights that much of what is put forward as globalization and/or Americanization is actually little more than 'globaloney' – about particular interests and the arguments that best advance them.

My main focus in the ensuing discussion of rugby relates to the cultural aspects of globalization (see especially, Tomlinson, 1999, 2007) and the ways in which different cultures intersect 'to produce new and distinctive hybrid forms that indicate continued or increasing heterogenization rather than the homogenization that is emphasized in the cultural convergence approach' (Ritzer, 2007: p. 13). As Houlihan (1994) has suggested while the tension between global and local cultures will be evident in terms of the organization of certain sports 'for the majority the tension will manifest itself in terms of particular sports' (p. 370). Any study attempting to engage with aspects of globalization and the intersection of local/global flows must do so with an appreciation and recognition of the subject 'in the round'. Trying to accomplish such a task is quite a challenge given the contested and somewhat nebulous use of terminology relating to globalization.

A good example of this would be the debates as to what constitutes the ages of globalization. Robertson's (1992) five-phase schema of globalization, which spans the fifteenth to twentieth centuries, is a widely cited source used to explain the advance of globalization and has been applied to football in his collaborative work with the sport sociologist Richard Giulianotti (Giulianotti and Robertson, 2009). Despite its presentation as something new, and a challenge to our very existence and identity at the local and/or national level, globalization has actually taken place for many years, as Robertson's (1992) outline makes clear. Robinson (2007) identifies three broad approaches to globalization. The first describes it as a process that has been going on since the dawn of history (5,000–10,000 year time frame). The second looks at globalization as a process coterminous with the spread of capitalism and modernity (500-year time frame). The third, focusing more on postmodernization, puts this in a 20–30 year time frame.

To clearly situate the present study it is important to emphasize that it deals primarily with the changes and development of rugby union since the game went openly professional. To this end much of the analysis and discussion engages with the third approach identified above and indeed considers professionalism as a key marker in the postmodernization of the sport (after Skinner, Stewart and Edwards, 2003). This is not to say that this process can be looked at in isolation and I will not try and explain the changes post-1995 while simultaneously ignoring the history and traditions of the game. Indeed, one of the central points made clear in the analysis is that professional rugby is often positioned as a visible symbol against tradition and, at times, the very virtues and essence of the game itself. The IRB (2008) outlines just what the game is meant to represent in their playing charter where they note that the game 'builds teamwork, understanding, co-operation and respect for fellow athletes' (p. 10). Yet the sheer speed of change from (sh)amateurism to professionalism meant that the sport was forced to alter at a much quicker rate than those administering the game, particularly in the northern hemisphere, could have ever imagined. Indeed, one of the key points that this work makes is that more than a decade on and the sport remains in a state of flux and continues to try and (re)define its place within the global sports arena. Chandler and Nauright (1996) noted that the control of the game and the changes within it 'have fallen within the purview of a very small group of people' (p. 246). Even with the seismic changes post 1995, and the shift from an ideology of amateurism to one governed by market forces and professionalism, little has changed in this regard. The postmodernization of rugby union in the professional age represents one of the central themes to the analysis presented in these pages and will form a part of the concluding section when I attempt to tie together much of what has happened to the sport since 1995 and offer some insights into where the game will go next as it continues to try and define its place within the global sports arena.

In an influential work on globalization the *New York Times* foreign affairs columnist Thomas Friedman (2000) assesses globalization as the conflict between the lexus and the olive tree. Without wishing to attempt to oversimplify, or indeed misrepresent, Friedman's central contention, I find his coupling useful in positioning amateurism and professionalism in rugby. Moreover, the coupling of the lexus and the olive tree gets to the heart of many of the tensions inherent within the often-stated dichotomy of the local and the global. As Friedman (2000: p. 31) notes:

> Olive trees are important. They represent everything that roots us, anchors us, identifies us and locates us in this world – whether it be belonging to a family, a community, a tribe, a nation, a religion or, most of all, a place called home.

Appadurai's (1996) notion of scapes is also very important here to highlight the ways in which various flows produce unique cultural realities around the world. Appadurai (1996) points to five scapes (global flows) that shape our social worlds. These ethnoscapes (flows of people), mediascapes (media flows), technoscapes (technological flows), financescapes (flows of money) and ideoscapes (flows of ideas) operate in fluid and irregular ways to (re)shape societies across the world (see also, Appadurai, 1990). Wallerstein's (1974) world systems theory has been utilized by a number of sports researchers to explain the movement of athletes from the periphery to the core. Yet it is also important to note that while the core and periphery are not always the same in sport as they are in wider economic terms these configurations also change markedly across sports. In the rugby world many nations that are part of the wider economic core of global affairs have a very marginal role on the periphery of the game. Indeed a great challenge for rugby in trying to develop as a truly global sport is that the power base and important decision-making is located within a very small group of nations.

Perhaps rugby's failure to embrace and engage with globalization is reflected by its absence in the majority of written works on the subject of sport and globalization, for in looking for examples to explain various global flows and the development of globalization in its widest sense rugby does not offer a particularly valuable reference point. In addition to the numerous journal articles on the subject, leading scholars in the sociology of sport have contributed texts on the relationship between sport and globalization (see for example, Bairner, 2001; Maguire, 1999; Miller et al., 2001; Van Bottenburg, 2001). Sport-specific studies on globalization issues as related to a particular activity have also furthered our understanding of the ways in which different sport forms engage with the various patterns and flows of the global age (e.g. Giulianotti and Robertson, 2009; Klein, 2006; Wagg, 2005). They reflect the shifting and contested arenas relating to globalization and in some ways may challenge conventional wisdom regarding core and periphery. Moreover, what may be the 'norm' in one sport is shown to be something quite the opposite in another. More than anything this highlights the dangers in making generalizations and applying particular theories and models to sport in a totalizing fashion when each individual activity is (re)construed and (re)constructed in very different ways. For what becomes clear as we attempt to look at the professionalization of rugby union and try to position this within and around discourses of globalization is that the picture it presents in many instances is that of a rather odd-shaped world. Nations that rarely figure in most discussions of globalization, such as New Zealand and Wales, hold a longstanding and exalted status in the rugby world. In determining the future of the game key decisions are made by men from a select group of nations who wield a substantial amount of power.

Roots and routes II: Structure of the book

While there has been much recent scholarship, including the book length analyses identified above, on sport and globalization it is noticeable that rugby is rarely considered in many discussions of global sport. Despite some notable exceptions (Chandler and Nauright, 1999; Nauright and Chandler, 1996; Ryan, 2008) there is little work on international rugby union – work focusing beyond studies of just one particular nation – and there is certainly a paucity of scholarship that engages fully with the complexities and variations that characterize the relationship between the global and the local in the game. Chapter 1 provides a brief overview of the game's origins and the development of the sport and then proceeds to present an outline of published litera-ture in the field highlighting some of the work undertaken by scholars into rugby union in specific countries across the globe.

In 1987 the first ever rugby world cup was held in New Zealand and Australia. This was significant for the ensuing discussions of the different interpretations of amateurism between nations and was a key marker in the eventual move to (open) professionalism that came after the 1995 competition in South Africa. Chapter 2 documents the development of the competition, and within this analysis considera-tion is given both to the relatively small number of countries who compete at the highest level of the sport and the politics involved in choosing who gets to host world cup competitions.

Chapter 3 considers how the move to open professionalism in rugby union signified something of a power shift in the relationship between the two codes of rugby and now rugby league ran the risk of losing some of its leading players to the union game. The open pro-fessionalization of rugby union changed the game in many countries and some of the leading rugby powers looked to recruit league players to the fifteen-man game (see Collins, 2006; Dunning and Sheard, 2005). The effects of this change may have been more marked in countries such as Wales and Australia who had seen many of their union internationals move to play rugby league during the century before open professionalism (Collins, 1998, 2006), and it is these two countries that form the focus of much of the chapter.

Recent years have witnessed a marked interest in the sporting celebrity (e.g. Andrews and Jackson, 2001; Smart, 2005). The increased commercialization and commmodification of rugby union has also seen a shift in the status of its athletes but rugby players have rarely been the feature of research by scholars looking at the sporting celebrity. Owing partly to the positioning of rugby as the 'national' sport in certain countries some players have achieved a profile beyond the game and so may be considered celebrities. Following a brief overview of what is meant by the term 'celebrity', Chapter 4 focuses on a number of players to look at how their profile may have repositioned the sport in other popular spheres. Players featured in this overview include Jonah Lomu of New Zealand, arguably the biggest star of the professional game to date; Jonny Wilkinson, whose match-winning drop goal in the 2003 world cup final cemented his status as a national icon in England; and Gavin Henson who became positioned as a celebrity for dating a famous singer (Harris and Clayton, 2007). Danny Cipriani of London Wasps and England is the latest player to undergo this extensive media focus and is featured in newspapers and magazines beyond the sports pages.

Alongside the growth of celebrity status for a select number of athletes, there has also been a marked increase in the migration of professional athletes. Association football has often been the focus of scholars given its undoubted position as the world's most popular sport (e.g. Giulianotti, 1999; Lanfranchi and Taylor, 2001; McGovern, 2002) but there has been relatively little work into the migration of rugby union players. Drawing upon previously published research on athlete migration, Chapter 5 provides some insights into the patterns of player migration in rugby during the professional age and attempts to tease out some of the key issues central to the increased internationalization of the game.

While much research has explored patterns of athlete migration (e.g. Bale, 1991; Lanfranchi and Taylor, 2001; Maguire, 1999) little work has looked at the migration of sports coaches. To date Wagg's (2007) study of two high-profile football coaches in England is one of the few works to look at the role of 'foreign' coaches in a national sport. Around the world various nations brought in overseas coaches both to their respective domestic games and to coach national rugby teams. In Chapter 6 I analyse the movement of rugby coaches and look at the relationships between different nations across the world in the contemporary game. Here the role of New Zealand coaches is particularly noteworthy for they continue to make a marked impact in the sport across a number of different places.

So, as stated above, while there has been a wealth of valuable research that has looked at the migration of athletes, in a whole host of sports, this has usually focused on the movement of players between clubs and little work has looked at the targeted identification of non-nationals to improve the performances of national teams. Chapter 7 analyses the conscious recruitment of overseas players to play for various nations in international rugby matches highlighting the complexity of national identity in professional rugby and the tensions between the local and the global in contemporary (re)presentations of the nation. Throughout the world players are actively recruited to represent national teams. Place of birth, (grand)parentage or residency criteria are used to decide eligibility and this issue offers an interesting point of departure to more closely consider the local and the global in a national context. Sameness and difference are explored when teasing out how certain non-national players are used as symbols to epitomize 'national character'. When a sport is used to (symbolically) represent the nation then this presents fertile ground for examining how global–local forces and tensions become manifest.

Rugby also offers an interesting site for exploring contemporary notions of British identity at a time when the very notion of Britishness seems under threat (e.g. Rojek, 2007; Weight, 2002). For a number of years there has been a British team, the Lions, or to give its full (but rarely used) title, the British and Irish Lions. The united Lions team offers an interesting means to consider the duality of national identity. After a brief overview of the history behind the touring team in Chapter 8, I look at the four Lions tours that have taken place since the game went professional. Within this analysis I look at how 'Britishness' is represented and how players may also remain Welsh, English, Irish and Scottish. It also offers further insights into the relationship between the home unions and the three rugby-playing nations that the team competes against (Australia, New Zealand and South Africa) in the southern hemisphere.

Engaging with Thomas Friedman's (2007) contention that 'the world is flat', the final chapter critically evaluates the current positioning of rugby and considers how the interplay of issues relating to localization and globalization impact upon the governance of the game. It discusses the most pressing problems and offers suggestions as to how the game may move forward. It develops an analysis of the glocal (Robertson, 1995) and the grobal (Ritzer, 2007) with specific reference to rugby union and critically assesses the postmodernization of the game and the changing nature of the sport in a professional age. Here I outline what I consider to be the footballization and Olympianization of rugby to further document the changes and challenges of the contemporary game. The local/global is presented as one of the core sociological dichotomies (Back, 1998) in a collection of works on the subject (Jenks, 1998). In sport, as Giulianotti and Robertson (2007) note in their use of the term 'glocalization', or as Andrews and Ritzer (2007) argue in their discussion of 'grobalization', rather than trying to view the local and the global as mutually exclusive the place of (a) sport is best contextualized by critically exploring the relationship between the two (see also, Jackson and Andrews, 1999).

So in terms of outlining and explaining just where 'the local' has been for me, to help locate some of the points made in framing this work and identifying the situated limits of my understanding, I hope that I have clearly positioned this text. Smith (2008: p. xi) is correct to assert that 'we all have a unique "take" on sport that means we experience it in an individual way'. While there is much discussion and debate about the various theoretical positioning informing sociological work on globalization, far less attention has been afforded to the location of the writer. As I see it, to be writing about anything, but particularly something that involves patterns of migration and the inter-relationship between different nations, the author must be writing from somewhere. The alternative, of course, is to be writing from nowhere (after Ritzer, 2007). Somewhere involves an appreciation and recognition of place – a subject that is very important in sport (Bale, 2003). The opposite of this is placelessness and it is hard to comprehend how we can even begin to try and understand globalization from such a vantage point. In finally moving to focus on the game itself there is really only one place that the story can start and it is to the town that gave the sport its name that I now turn.

1
Where and Why Rugby Matters

The sport of rugby union takes its name from a town in the middle of England. I lived there for a period in the mid-1990s and from the plaque at Rugby School which states how in 1823 William Webb Ellis 'with a fine disregard for the rules of football as played in his time, first took the ball in his arms and ran with it', to the museum where you could watch a rugby ball being hand stitched, this is largely what gives this small town its identity. The areas surrounding Rugby are those where association football is, just like in most other parts of the country, the dominant sport. England's second city, Birmingham, is home to two premier league football teams, and other major football clubs are nearby. Living in the shadow of the association game is a constant of much of the history of rugby both before and during the professional age. Nearby Coventry were once a formidable power in English rugby but by the dawn of the professional age had witnessed years of decline and languished below the top-tier of the game (A. Smith, 1999). Within this chapter I briefly outline the history of the game and then provide a broad overview of where and why rugby matters. This is intended to serve as an introduction to better locate the sport in a wider perspective and provide some context to the discussion that follows.

The origins of rugby union

Rugby union, like its sister code of association football, evolved from the variants of folk football that were a characteristic of pre-industrialized Britain. These games were very much local affairs as each particular

11

place played their game in something of a splendid isolation. Indeed, confusion over the different rules and terminology were a defining feature of the 'football' contests of this period and even after the codification of these games following the 'split' of 1863 it was not uncommon for teams turning up to play an association football match to find that their opponents were a rugby football team (Garland, 1993).

Prior to this it was in the public schools of England that the games first became subject to more stringent controls and regulation in the mid-1800s (Dunning and Sheard, 1979). It was at Rugby School in 1845 that the first laws were written down and its origins within the public school system served as a powerful symbol of manliness, masculinity and muscular Christianity (Nauright and Chandler, 1996). These rules were then taken to the leading universities by the students from the school and then as these old Rugbeians graduated and became school masters they were taken to other schools (many of whom already had their own form of 'football'). This of course is a very short and incomplete explanation of the early development of rugby (as a codified sport) as space does not permit a detailed discussion of this process but the work of social historians clearly outline these developments elsewhere (see especially, Collins, 2009; Dunning and Sheard, 1979; Nauright and Chandler, 1996).

There is little evidence to support the place of Webb Ellis as the central figure in the development of rugby football and in an age where oral testimony held sway it is important to note that Thomas Hughes, author of the influential *Tom Brown's Schooldays*, attended Rugby School in the 1830s and that the Webb Ellis legend had not survived a little more than a decade after the now widely celebrated event was said to have occurred. In 1923 a combined Wales-England team played an Ireland-Scotland team on the very field where Webb Ellis 'picked up the ball' to commemorate the occasion and thus further reinforce its status as the significant moment in the birth of the game. Sixty-four years on and the Webb Ellis Cup was the most coveted prize in the game as the sport took what we can now recognize as an inevitable step towards open professionalism.

Whatever the exact sequence of events in the development of the sport of rugby union, and the merits of the claim from those associated with the Rugby School, Webb Ellis has become an important figure in the game. Like many other sports it is hard to clearly define who actually 'invented' the game for there is evidence of games with characteristics resembling rugby dating back centuries (Dunning and Sheard, 2005). What cannot be disputed though is that the games were codified in England and in the case of rugby and cricket transported to parts of the British Empire. As Andrews and Grainger (2007: p. 484) note, 'Britain's imperial and commercial hegemony during the nineteenth century facilitated the global spread and legitimation of the modern sport forms developed within the British context' (see also, van Bottenburg, 2001). As I discuss in Chapter 8 much of the discourse couched in British terms really refers largely to England and at times it is hard to separate the two. The significance of Rugby School is important here for the games developed at the institution, and others like it, were exported by the public schoolboys as they moved on to university and to professional careers. The story of Webb Ellis also offers a comforting reference point in discourses of nostalgia. Sean Smith (1999: p. 21) capably shows the importance of the story and notes:

> The beauty of Webb Ellis as an historical tool for the elitist controllers of rugby was that, while it is nearly impossible to prove that he invented rugby in its modern form, it is absolutely impossible to prove that he didn't.

Nostalgia is an important concept in contemporary rugby for it helps remind us of the way things used to be and provides a reassuring link to the past. According to Keating (1993: p. 5) 'any half-decent sport has to be a sucker for nostalgia'. For Jameson (1991) nostalgia is an attempt to lay siege either to our own present and immediate past or to a more distant history that escapes individual existential memory. Maguire (1994: p. 413) notes how 'closely linked to nostalgia is a sense of melancholy, a longing for a time, a place'. As we begin to explore the relationship between the past, the present and the future in rugby union it is clear that nostalgia has always been an integral part of the sport and that it is used as a tool to resist change and provide cultural security (see also, Nauright, 1994). Much of the media coverage of rugby during the summer of 2009 made references back to the amateur era and highlighted how the many changes to the game in the professional age had fundamentally altered the very ethos of the sport. In nostalgic recollections of a romantic past many writers sought refuge by commenting on the ills of football in their critiques of the professional rugby world. This suggested 'footballization' of rugby is a point I will consider in the final chapter of this book.

Locating rugby: Core and periphery

In attempting to look at the relationship of the sport of rugby union to contemporary discourses of globalization it is also important to note that there are only a few countries where the game has any type of significant presence. In a report titled *Putting Rugby First* some concerned rugby supporters outlined the challenges facing the game today:

> Rugby's main issue is its narrow global footprint: its popularity is largely limited to the Foundation Unions – eight relatively small countries. Rugby is not played or followed, to any significant degree, in the large and fast growing nations that will be the engines of the world's future economic growth.
>
> (Spectrum Value Partners and
> Addleshaw Goddard, 2008: p. 3)

These eight nations have assumed a hegemonic role in the governance of the game and a small number of these have also been the dominant nations on the field of play. The four home unions (Wales, Scotland, Ireland and England) and France have dominated the game in the northern hemisphere and despite the addition of Italy to form a Six Nations championship in 2000, the power base remains in the old Five Nations. In the southern hemisphere, South Africa, New Zealand and Australia have assumed a similar status to the five nations highlighted above; although it is also important to note that in the international sphere these southernmost nations have been the dominant playing powers of the professional era. We can view these eight nations as a collective, and very powerful, core but it is also useful to view them as two separate geographic cores when moving on to critically analyse the sport in relation to globalization. Of course the importance of empire and the colonial roots of the game is also key here for the dominant nations all share the English language with France being the exception to the norm in this respect (S. Smith, 1999). In Wallerstein's (1974) widely used world-systems approach, based on a neo-Marxist critique of globalization, it is stated that there is a core and a periphery. The idea of a semi-periphery is also invoked here and it would be an appropriate term to describe the place of nations such as Argentina and Italy in rugby for they are increasingly moving closer to the core yet still do not receive the voting rights of the eight foundation unions in the international governance process. Yet such is the dominance of the eight core nations in all aspects of the sport, I generally refer to just the core and the periphery throughout most of the text even though it is clear that certain nations are closer to the core than others. It is also important to note that while acknowledging the work of Wallerstein (1974), and employing this terminology of core and periphery, I am in no way claiming to (mis)represent his thesis and simply apply this to rugby. The language of core and periphery seems an appropriate one to apply to the international rugby landscape but beyond that I make no other claims to invoke Wallerstein's (1974) analysis into the present discussion.

This narrow core at the heart of world rugby is one of the reasons why the game will continue to struggle to develop its profile and positioning within the broader sporting and cultural landscape. It is rather easy to predict, with some confidence, which eight teams will make up the quarter-finalists at the quadrennial world cup competition. Many would also be confident of identifying the three or four nations that would have a genuine hope of winning the competition even though the International Rugby Board (2004) has a stated aim of ten nations capable of reaching the world cup final come 2015. Since 1999, the first world cup finals in the age of open professionalism, only ten nations have featured in the quarterfinals of the tournament. The three largest economies among the top eight nations are France, England and Australia. Collectively, they make up five of the six finalists during the professional age highlighting how professionalism 'favours the rich and the numerous' (Richards, 2007: p. 288). In 2007 Argentina became the first team from outside the eight foundation unions to advance to the semi-finals of the competition. In fact during the whole history of the tournament only 22 nations have competed in the finals. This contrasts markedly to the FIFA World Cup where in the same period 56 different nations have taken part in the finals. Argentina's success might also be construed as occurring in spite of, rather than as a result of, any strategic development initiatives from those involved in the governance of the international game.

Few countries would claim rugby as their national sport. Of the foundation unions of the IRB, Wales and New Zealand are nations whose very identities are implicitly tied to their respective national XVs (Richards, 2005; Ryan, 1993; Smith and Williams, 1980). Anderson's (1983) conception of 'imagined communities' is also important to acknowledge here. As I have previously noted with regard to rugby in Wales (Harris, 2007), and various scholars point out with reference to the game in New Zealand (e.g. Falcous and West, 2009; Hope, 2002; Scherer and Jackson, 2008), the sport can serve an important symbolic function as a means of uniting the nation. Yet it is sometimes wrongly surmised that just because something is imagined it is imaginary. Bairner (2009) has clearly highlighted how the nation, sport and landscape are interconnected texts and that despite some ambiguity as to what is real and/or imagined 'the nation has material substance' (p. 225). Hobsbawm (1991: p. 142) famously commented that 'the imagined community of millions seems more real as a team of eleven named people' to explain the hegemonic positioning of association football across the globe but in Wales and New Zealand it is a fifteen-man version of football that occupies an exalted position. In a more recent work Hobsbawm (2007) again refers to association football to further highlight the scope of this sport and its significance in the dialectics of the relations between globalization, national identity and xenophobia. Rugby's reach and appeal may not be anywhere close to that of football but while claims to its apparent globalization are somewhat exaggerated it is a sport that is developing in the international arena. The IRB (2004) state as much in their strategic plan noting the growth of membership over the previous decade but also acknowledging that 'there are many issues which must be tackled ... if rugby is to consolidate its base and reach out to become a truly global sport' (p. 2).

Of course the use of sport as a marker of national identity and as a means of imagining the nation is not as straightforward as often presented. For the small Pacific island of Fiji it is the seven-a-side version of the sport that is more prominent. Although rugby in Wales may be an integral part of this (re)imaging and (re)imagining (Harris, 2008), it is only really in the south of the country that the game matters. It is not just geography that is important to note here; for many years rugby was firmly positioned as the white man's game and the sport of the Afrikaners in South Africa (Black and Nauright, 1998; Carlin, 2008).

Moreover in most parts of the world rugby is very much positioned as a man's game (see especially, Nauright and Chadler, 1996) and women's participation in the sport remains something of a contested ideological terrain. Indeed, the recent promotion of women's rugby often largely influenced by wider discourses of 'equity', stated agendas of social inclusion or more pertinently the increased funding that comes with such rhetoric, shows that they have been a marginalized group for many years. To this end women's rugby has been helped enormously by the push to have Rugby Sevens included in the Olympic Games where part of the criteria on deciding which of the bidding sports to include centred on the governing body demonstrating that the sport can be an activity that has participants of both sexes. For after years of neglect, the International Olympic Committee (IOC), just like the IRB and numerous other governing bodies of sport, are finally taking an interest in women's sport and attempting to redress years of indifference and inequality. A key point overlooked in this newfound equity discussion and celebration is that by and large the developments being undertaken are those that are trying to mimic the already established and exalted male versions of the sport. These established traditions need neither the prefix 'men' nor are they being measured against any other form of the game whereas the women's version is always positioned as the other. As Hargreaves (1994) has noted, the challenge for such development is that although being incorporated into wider male structures may result in women gaining access to better resources, in doing so they may relinquish control of their own game.

Yet in real terms, for women and men, in much of the world rugby does not matter. As the *Putting Rugby First* report notes there are less than a quarter of a million players in the ten most populated nations in the world (Spectrum Value Partners and Addleshaw Goddard, 2008). Over half of all registered players in the world are in England and three-quarters of all registered players are from the eight foundation unions. In this sense the sport still remains tied to its colonial roots and has a very limited global appeal.

An eight-man shove: Maintaining possession

The focus of this work is on rugby union since 1995. Given its particular focus and the obvious limitations of space I will not go into a detailed history of the origins of the game or its development before 1995. This has already been well documented in relation to the hegemonic core (S. Smith, 1999) and in relation to the wider rugby-playing world (Richards, 2007). In the next section I identify key texts that form the base upon which all further works were developed and then refer to some of the important research undertaken in relation to rugby to date within specific nations. Much of this literature is drawn from the sociology of sport although I also incorporate work outside of this and also make reference to sports history scholarship, research from the field of sports management and wider works from a variety of other disciplines.

Dunning and Sheard's (1979) *Barbarians, Gentlemen and Players* provided an important moment in the academic study of the sport. Written from an Eliasian process sociological perspective the authors outline the development of the game within the context of the 'civilizing process' that forms a central tenet of Elisian thinking. Using figurational sociology to explain how the sport developed in England, Dunning and Sheard (1979) clearly outline the influence of social class, the inherent regional tensions and the changing culture of the game. One year after this book was published the social historians Dai Smith and Gareth Williams (1980) wrote the official history of the Welsh Rugby Union (WRU). *Fields of Praise* is not only considered to be one of the most important books written about rugby but was a key text within sports history in general.

Books aimed at a more layman readership have also added much to our understanding of the impact of professionalism in recent years (e.g. Jones, 2000; Malin, 1997; McRae, 2007; Nicholls, 2006). In this genre the readable *A Game for Hooligans* (Richards, 2007) attempts to fill a void in the literature for the author notes that not since James and Reason (1979) published *The World of Rugby* has there been an English language text that details a general history of the game although Johnson's (2000) irreverent history often gets overlooked. S. Smith's (1999) book *The Union Game*, which accompanies a BBC television series of the same name, is also an important work to note here in providing a concise and clear overview of the game in the core nations. That English is the language spoken most widely in seven of the eight core nations in the game, with France being the exception to the norm in this regard, powerfully illustrates the roots of the game. However, this is not to say that work on world rugby has not been published in other languages, such as that of Bodis (1987), yet much of this work has not had the audience it deserves in many of the leading rugby-playing nations.

Collins (2009) provides one of the most cognizant explanations of the social and cultural positioning of rugby in a particular country. Here the centrality of class-based ideologies to the social and cultural positioning of rugby union is outlined to clearly explain the place of rugby in English society. Smith (2000) offers a pertinent and informed analysis of the challenges facing the sport in England following the move to an openly professional game that clearly outlines the power struggles between the various factions (see also, Malcolm, Sheard and White, 2000; O'Brien and Slack, 2004). As self-styled guardians of the game the RFU are central to both the advances made in the expansion of the sport and the barriers erected to hamper progress. Of particular interest in this is the relationship of the RFU with all other national governing bodies in the sport where they have had a contentious and at times quite strained relationship throughout the history of the game. England's failed bid to host the 2007 world cup is a recent example to highlight that this shows little signs of abating even in the professional era. The fact that the organization does not require a prefix of which nation it represents is a visible symbol of its hegemonic status and primacy in the history of the game. That the RFU refused to be part of the original International Rugby Board (then named the International Rugby Football Board) where it was left to Ireland, Scotland and Wales to draw up an agreed upon framework for the game also offers a pertinent pointer to some of the challenges impacting upon the development of the sport in the long term.

If England is the birthplace and ancestral 'home' of modern rugby then New Zealand is often considered to be the game's spiritual home. In New Zealand Greg Ryan has done much to improve our understanding of the early history of the game (Ryan, 1993). Reflecting its status as the national sport many other academics either born in, or working out of, New Zealand have written on aspects of the game focusing in large part on identity politics and the branding of the All Blacks (e.g. Falcous and West, 2009; Hope, 2002; Jackson, Batty and Scherer, 2001; Jackson and Hokowhitu, 2002; Scherer and Jackson, 2008). In a nation where rugby is so important then there are of course a number of other works on the game both within the academic literature and that aimed at a more popular market. Much of this will be touched upon in the subsequent chapters when I look at specific issues such as the migration of coaches and players (e.g. Chiba and Jackson, 2006; Howitt and Haworth, 2002). Another key issue relating to rugby in the country surrounds its long-standing rivalry with South Africa.

Black and Nauright (1998) provide a detailed insight into the positioning of rugby in South Africa that shows many of the challenges faced in developing the sport and trying to move beyond its image as a symbol of apartheid. While South African sport as a whole spent much of the latter part of the twentieth century excluded from international events, the rugby community was less averse to continuing links, and 'amateur' players could receive a healthy remuneration for being part of so-called rebel tours there. When the country was officially welcomed back into the rugby world and awarded the 1995 world cup finals, then it quickly reassumed its place as a leading nation in the game. Few sporting events have ever been as significant to a nation than the 1995 Rugby World Cup was to South Africa (Carlin, 2008) and I will touch upon this in the next chapter as I look at the significance of the competition on the road to open professionalism.

With the exception of Hickie's (1993) excellent work, rugby's position in Australia has perhaps been less well defined than in the two nations above given the hegemonic status of rugby league and Australian Rules football within the sporting landscape. Horton (2009) has outlined how the sport remains a particularly 'glocal' game within the country. His analysis cogently outlines the dominance of Sydney as the centre of the sport in the country and reminds us that although national labels can be ascribed to sports more often than not it is a particular city or region that plays a key role in a certain activity. The interrelationships between these places form an important connectivity in the global age and will be considered later in the text when considering whether we are seeing a 'flattening' of the rugby world.

Australia's rivalry with their neighbours New Zealand forms another important aspect of the game in the southern hemisphere. In 2008 these nations met each other in Hong Kong to contest the Bledisloe Cup. Aside from world cup matches this was the first time that the two teams had squared off against each other outside their respective countries and generated much needed revenue for both unions.

A 2009 Bledisloe Cup contest was penciled in for the US although this was subsequently changed to Japan. The US and Japan represent two key sites in any discussions of the globalization of rugby and the Americanization and Asianization of the game over the next decade are obvious areas for targeted growth and development.

The role of sport as an important marker of national pride and identity in the Celtic nations has been well documented (e.g. Jarvie and Walker, 1994; Johnes, 2005; Sugden and Bairner, 1993). Reflecting both the broader landscape of the sociology of sport, and its positioning in the country, there is much more published work on football than there is on rugby in Scotland. Academic work on rugby in Ireland is also rather scarce; although Tuck's (2003) research provides key insights into the dynamics surrounding the sport as a symbol of national identity, for unlike in many other sports Ireland compete as one nation in international rugby union (see also, Tuck and Maguire, 1999). The work of social historians has clearly explained the landscape of sport in Wales and the distinctive place of rugby within this (e.g. Johnes, 2005; Smith and Williams, 1980; Williams, 1991). Howe's (1999, 2001) research is a valuable case study of both the importance of rugby in a south Wales community and also the challenges caused by open professionalism to the distinctive habitus of the club.

So of the eight foundation unions of the IRB the seven nations briefly referred to above are either British or former British colonies. The 'odd-man out' in this collective of eight is France although its close proximity to England helps explain the place of rugby here (Dine, 2001). Pierre de Coubertin, founder of the modern Olympics, provides a pertinent example of how the geographic proximity to England and the ethos of muscular Christianity saw these English influences impact upon sport in France. Rugby featured in the Olympics as early as 1900 and de Coubertin was one of the first inductees into the IRB Hall of Fame in 2007. Influenced by the games played at Rugby School, which he had visited, de Coubertin was regarded as one of the pioneers of the French game. Rugby's place in the Olympic Games became an important issue again much more recently and the potential significance of its return to the games will be considered later on. In the English language, Philip Dine is the leading authority on rugby in France and has provided an insightful commentary on the sport in that country (Dine, 2001). The move to an openly professional game and a resultant shift in the local/global interface has been assessed in relation to rugby in France (Augustin, 1999). Here it is noted that the open professionalization of rugby and its associated economic and media-led imperatives have cast doubt on the stability of traditional sport systems and resulted in a marked change in the social and cultural position of rugby clubs anchored in specific localities. All nations, inside and outside of the core, will have felt this impact from the twin processes of globalization and open professionalism.

The brief treatise above, like much of the text, focuses on a small group of nations. Those becoming more involved in the core of the game such as Italy, Argentina and Samoa feature in parts but a number of nations who play the sport do so in a world far removed from those nations identified above and thus have had little written about them. If rugby is to develop and become more international then it is hoped that future works will be able to document these advances and that accounts will be published concerning those nations who are furthest out on the periphery of the game. It is important to note here that these nations include big and small nations, rich and poor places, and are located in all parts of the world. When you look beyond the core it is clear that rugby faces numerous challenges in developing its profile as other (sometime competing) sports are already well established in these places. The aesthetics of the game may also be a burden in this regard. As Horton (2009: pp. 968–9) has highlighted:

> Rugby's unique form, its uncompromisingly violent nature, its highly complex set of 'laws' and its subtext of heroism, selflessness and camaraderie have made it a game that only the 'committed' could appreciate.

Van Bottenburg (2001) has noted that the game's limited appeal across most of continental Europe due to its two faces – 'rough yet elitist' (p. 115) – meant that it has always struggled to find a widespread audience. The push to develop Rugby Sevens and in particular the successful campaign to have this sport included in the Olympic Games in 2016 is an important development to note here.

Chronicling the rugby world

While there have been a number of authored and edited collections on aspects of world football (e.g. Armstrong and Giulianotti, 2001;

Giulianotti, 1999; Giulianotti and Robertson, 2009; Goldblatt, 2008; Lanfranchi and Taylor, 2001; Murray, 1998; Wagg, 1984, 1995) far less attention has been afforded to rugby union. Nauright and Chandler's (1996) collection on rugby and masculine identity is one of the few texts to critically explore the importance of rugby in a number of places. Featuring examples from Australia, England, New Zealand, South Africa and Wales the contributors to this collection outline how rugby became an important tool in promoting notions of manliness. Chandler and Nauright (1999) followed this up three years later with another collection that expanded on the above to include further analysis of race, gender and commerce. In this second book the contributors also look to Italy, Japan and the US although the bulk of the collection still focuses on case studies of the game in parts of Britain and its former colonies. More recently Ryan (2008) edited a collection of essays that looked at the professionalization of the sport in different parts of the rugby-playing world. Ryan's (2008) anthology offers an important contribution to better understanding how different nations have dealt with the move to open professionalism. This book contains essays by scholars on a number of the leading rugby nations and the only noticeable omission is that there is no chapter on Argentina. Argentina represents a particularly interesting case to consider local-global intersections within the international rugby sphere and it is a subject I will return to in Chapter 5. Ryan's (2008) collection provides a useful resource in developing some of the ideas I consider in this book and offers a timely evaluation of the impacts of professionalism across leading rugby nations. Yet all the works referred to above still leave space to further explore relationships between these different nations and this is the prime focus of my work here.

In writing about the New Zealand All Blacks, arguably the most iconic 'brand' in all of rugby (Gilson et al., 2000; Jackson, Batty and Scherer, 2001), the geographers Lewis and Winder (2007) note that despite the presence of Coca Cola and Adidas 'the "globalization" of rugby still occurs largely within empire, issues of professionalization continue to haunt the game, governance is locally specific and rugby still relies upon national representative teams to build brand attachments' (pp. 203–4). This quote concisely highlights the challenges that are at the heart of the focus of this book in terms of offering a critique of rugby's failure to embrace globalization and considering what has and can be done to expand the game.

It was not until 1987 that the first rugby world cup was staged. This came almost a century after the beginning of the modern Olympics and close to 60 years after the first ever football world cup. Rugby's failure to develop as a global game is evidenced by the venues chosen for this tournament and the limited number of nations taking part. Indeed, as the guardians of the game are finally claiming to be 'reaching out' it is an interesting time to consider how and where they are doing this. Of course the desire to reach out is guided by the forces of consumer capitalism and the quest to develop the sport beyond the relatively narrow confines of its existing core. The successful campaign to get Rugby Sevens admitted into the Olympic Games is clearly very important here although it remains to be seen whether the impact of this will actually be anything close to what the celebratory discourse surrounding it has initially proposed.

If the inception of the rugby world cup in 1987 provided the early tentative steps on the path to open professionalism (Grundlingh, 1995) then the catalyst was the 1995 event in South Africa eight years later where professionalism became an inevitable consequence of increasing media involvement in the game. It was there that the three southern hemisphere countries of the foundation unions announced that they had agreed to a ten-year deal with Rupert Murdoch's News Corporation worth $555 million dollars. Black and Nauright (1998) have noted that while the 1995 world cup did not cause the shift into open professionalism 'it did provide a decisive push to the steadily expanding commercialization of the sport which had been gathering steam since the first world cup in 1987' (p. 137). The next chapter looks at the importance of the rugby world cup as a key marker in the internationalization of the game. Hutchins (1998) suggests that the initiation and ongoing staging of the tournament 'represents a formal re-configuring of rugby's economic and cultural politics' (p. 38). The next chapter considers the importance of the rugby world cup in relation to the development of the sport.

2
The Rugby World Cup

I was in high school when the first rugby world cup took place and I remember getting up at 5a.m. to turn on the television and watch Wales play. As highlighted in the previous chapter, the sport has a particularly narrow global footprint so the very fact that rugby followers in more than half of the leading nations taking part would have a similar wake-up time to watch the games should be noted. Such a scenario would seem hard to imagine now. If at all possible the kick-off times of matches at major sporting events are scheduled so that viewers in the most important television markets are not inconvenienced and, more importantly, that commercial partners are able to reach their target markets. In the 2008 Olympic Games the times of the gymnastics and swimming events in Beijing were scheduled to satisfy the USA television market. A year before this, two European boxers fought a championship bout in front of 50,000 fans in the Millennium Stadium, Cardiff, that did not start until 1a.m. local time.

Increasingly, sporting events while still being promoted to 'local' paying spectators who attend the contest are also being (re)configured for global television audiences. Major sporting events are the most important spectacles here with the increased commercialization and commodification of elite sport making these a prime symbol of globalization (Roche, 2000). Global brands compete for the rights to act as official sponsors of these events that promise extensive reach and entry into international television markets across continents (Amis and Cornwell, 2005). In this regard international sport offers something that no other element of popular culture can and serves as an important commercial tool in the twenty-first century. The FIFA world cup finals are the marker for all other sports here for through global television this sport has been 'transformed into a worldwide capitalist industrial complex' (Hobsbawm, 2007: p. 90) and is something that many other sports, including rugby, look at with envy.

Yet what the above also shows is just how amateur rugby union was in 1987. This is not meant in a derogatory fashion although it is interesting to note that now discourse of the amateur has taken on the same negative connotation that was once attached to the word professional in a number of sporting contexts (Allison, 2001; Smith and Porter, 2000). Smith (2008) notes how 'amateur' was for many years a compliment to someone who played solely for the love of the game but now 'amateurism has become a byword for sloppiness, disorganization and ineptitude' (p. 13). The first rugby world cup was described as the largest amateur sporting event of all time. The 16 teams that competed in the inaugural event were all invited – there was no qualification process to allow all nations the opportunity to take part. Matches took place in the day, often at times inconvenient both for television audiences in other parts of the world and for those planning on actually attending the games. But there were also practical reasons for this as few stadiums had floodlights and those involved in the governance of the game had not yet really grasped just what could be achieved (Wyatt, 1996).

In this chapter I consider the role of the rugby world cup as a key marker in the developing internationalization of the sport and an important step on the road to open professionalism. It highlights how the inception of a world cup competition marked an important step on the path to rugby becoming an openly professional game and highlights how in a very short period, by the time the third event took place, the end of (sh)amateurism became an inevitable outcome of a battle for control of the game between media forces. So as outlined before, while the main focus of the text is rugby in the professional era it is important to take a step back at times and explain the history and context of how things were different (and similar) in the period prior to 1995 to better locate the analysis of contemporary issues.

Locating rugby in the wider international sporting landscape

When we begin to compare the profile and positioning of rugby union against other sports it is clear that the game lags far behind many others in terms of having an international appeal and wide scope of participants and spectators. In contemporary times football is often used as the model upon which all other sports should base their commercial development and, as I will discuss later, was, in England at least, cited as the model whereby many rich benefactors first became involved in the game. Yet rugby is not football and can in no way match the truly global reach of a sport that is easier to play and much simpler to understand (Giulianotti and Robertson, 2009). Such a comparison between the two is unfair on many levels but in beginning to critically assess rugby's global positioning it is important to note how the rugby world cup 'fits' within and around other major sporting events. In his work on the development of modern sport Dunning (1999) notes how the early development of the association game was based on identifying itself as different from rugby. Much of the discussion of rugby union in the professional era is based upon comparative analyses, for good and for bad, with the global game of football. There are many references to football throughout this text and in the final chapter I consider whether we are seeing a 'footballization' of rugby.

The first modern Olympics took place in 1896 and the first football world cup took place in 1930. The Olympics (Summer) and the football world cup are without doubt the two biggest sporting events on the planet. What scholars often refer to as 'mega-events' (Horne and Manzenreiter, 2006; Roberts, 2004; Roche, 2000) now dominate the sporting landscape. Roberts (2004) notes that the lines are blurred and that 'some megas are bigger than others' (p. 109). Roche (2000) has described mega-events as large-scale cultural events 'which have a dramatic character, mass popular appeal and international significance' (p. 1). These events will attract widespread media coverage and may have significant impacts on the host city/region (Horne and Manzenreiter, 2006; Roche, 2000). Preuss (2004) has clearly outlined that the economic impact of hosting a major sporting event varies markedly across time and place. While few would dispute the hegemonic positioning of the Olympic Games and the football world cup there is still some debate as to what other sporting competitions can lay claim to being truly 'mega' events.

After the two big mega sporting events many other competitions, including the rugby world cup, now compete for the title of the third biggest sports event in the world. Claim and counter-claim as to what is the third biggest sporting event in the world are visible across sport with the bi-annual Ryder Cup golf competition and the European football championships among those adopting this position. The IRB (2009) also stake a claim to this although the relatively narrow reach of the game and its failure to develop within many of the largest economies and population bases makes this somewhat problematic. The special place of the Super Bowl in American culture means that this is also often promoted and perceived as a major international event although the reality is that outside the US the worldwide viewing figures for this game are not as high as often suggested. Indeed the claims of all the aforementioned, when it relates to television viewing figures, are based on some tenuous and at times confusing assumptions. Perhaps in an attempt to be considered 'mega', or to increase the amount of sponsorship dollars they can seek, inflated figures are claimed for a range of international sporting competitions. The gap between the estimated and the confirmed viewing figures fluctuate for most sporting events and the difference between the two figures are sometimes millions (or even billions) apart. The IRB (2008) claims that 119 different nations screened coverage of the finals providing the possibility of a cumulative reach of 4.2 billion people for the 2007 competition. A more accurate figure notes that 33 million people watched the final of the tournament and that of this number 97 per cent were from the eight foundation unions (Spectrum Value Partners and Addleshaw Goddard, 2008). This would be just a fraction of the number of Americans who tuned in to the Super Bowl of that year. While considerable doubt remains surrounding the television audience for this and other major sporting events it is clear that the rugby world cup has grown exponentially in the 20 years it had been in existence up to and including the 2007 event in France.

Quite why those governing rugby did not start a world cup competition until 1987 is easy to explain. In part it was a reflection of the fact that very few countries had embraced the game and that those small group of countries who governed the sport expressed no great desire to export it and see the game develop elsewhere. Even through the professional age issues concerning ownership of the game and a desire to retain power and prestige are omnipresent. It was also a reflection of amateurism in that arranging time off work and lengthy periods away from home could be quite problematic for some players. Many, though certainly not all, international rugby players actually lost money by pursuing international honours in the game. With the home nations very much at the core of the rugby-playing world then, there was a real reluctance to share the game with other nations. A fear of being beaten at their own game seemed to loom large in the minds of rugby's administrators. The Rugby Football Union (RFU) in England saw themselves as guardians of the game and in particular the ethos of amateurism (Collins, 2009). A tour to the southern hemisphere by the British and Irish Lions team had been undertaken since the 1880s (Thomas, 2005) and for many in the home unions was considered to be internationalization enough for the sport.

Wyatt (1996) suggests that the fact that a world cup competition took place at all 'was some kind of minor miracle' (p. 21) given the animosity that existed between the home unions and the other four members of the IRB. Moreover the home unions were often involved in disputes and petty squabbles among themselves. Throughout the history of the game matches had been cancelled and relations temporarily ceased due to debates concerning payment of players and other such controversies surrounding interpretations of amateurism (S. Smith, 1999).

The name of the trophy itself, the Webb Ellis Cup, provided an important link to the history and origins of the sport. Of course, as highlighted previously, the myth of Webb Ellis remains a contested explanation for the origins of the game but serves well to provide a reassuring link to a nostalgic past. To all intents and purposes the competitors at the first world cup were amateur players. Yet for many of the northern hemisphere players it was apparent early on that the sport's amateur regulations and interpretations of professionalism were quite different in New Zealand in particular. The injured New Zealand captain Andy Dalton appeared in television commercials advertising tractors. Of course it was his status as captain of the national team in the national sport that afforded him such a contract yet to conform to IRB regulations the caption that accompanied the advert read 'Andy Dalton – farmer'. Perhaps more than anything it was the inception of a world cup competition that paved the way towards open professionalism. This statement does not underestimate the role of the media for ultimately it was a battle for control of the game by media magnates that forced the sport into open professionalism

(Fitzsimons, 1996). Yet in 1987 the amateur ethos of the game was still visible in many respects and few would have predicted that the sport was on the cusp of professionalism (Wyatt, 1996). Wales, for example, when beset by injuries called up a nineteen-year-old prop forward who happened to be holidaying nearby. Grundlingh (1995) notes that once the sport, though still officially amateur, committed itself to the world of agents and advertisers 'the game, the players, and its administration could never be the same again' (p. 19).

Hutchins (1998) has looked at the role of the earliest rugby world cups in the increased globalization of the sport (see also Hutchins and Phillips, 1999). Hutchins and Phillips (1999) highlight how 1987 was chosen as the year for the first rugby world cup tournament so as not to clash with the Olympic Games, scheduled to take place in Seoul, South Korea in 1988, and the football world cup taking place in Italy during the summer of 1990. What this work only acknowledges in an endnote is that the British and Irish Lions were scheduled to tour Australia in 1989. This was a more important factor than often acknowledged in deciding when to stage the first world cup (Wyatt, 1996). Australia and New Zealand were more ready to stage the inaugural competition. In the bumpy path to professionalism then it is clear that the southern hemisphere nations were more progressive and better prepared for an open game than their counterparts in the north. As the journalist Stephen Jones (2000: p. 31) noted in comparing the development of the professional game in two different parts of the world:

> Here's the southern hemisphere approach to sorting out a format for top rugby for a professional season. Get a tiny group of power-brokers together. Serve coffee. Sort it. Leave. Here's the northern approach. Flap around helplessly for five years in a cesspool of ill-feeling, self-aggrandisement, self-interest and incompetence, wasting priceless opportunities. And still fail.

Wyatt's (1996) text offers an illuminating insight into the politicking involved in the inception of an international competition for the sport. Throughout the history of the game disputes and agendas loom large with a small power elite exerting considerable influence over the sport. Yet this was not a problem just confined to rugby, for issues surrounding the voting for hosting a major sporting event and concerns relating to bribery and corruption seem to form a staple part of sport governance in the international arena (see especially, Jennings, 1996, 2006; Sugden and Tomlinson, 1998).

In rugby much of the politicking stemmed from the relations between members of the four home unions. They rarely agreed with each other and often fell out with France. The relationship between these core European nations and the leading rugby nations in the southern hemisphere was also a fraught one and the whole history of the game features conflict between these eight nations. Given the centrality of class-related ideologies dominant in England, and also in the other home nations, at times there was a real disdain for what they saw as the attitude of colonial upstarts who should have known their place. The four home unions saw themselves as the rulers of the game and once again there are interesting comparisons to be made between these attitudes and that of their football counterparts some 50 years previously, who looked on with some bemusement as the first world cup was contested. Collectively the eight foundation unions had, according to Wyatt (1996), 'strangled rugby' fearing that if they democratized the sport 'they would lose control or that other countries would beat them at their own game' (p. 52). New Zealand were the first ever world champions defeating France in the final and playing an exciting brand of rugby that clearly demonstrated just how far ahead they were of many of the leading northern hemisphere nations in particular. What the event also highlighted, and something that was to resurface time and again at some of the later tournaments, was the massive gulf in playing standards with many teams outside the core finding themselves subject to humiliating defeats.

The 1991 event took place in the northern hemisphere and despite the recommendation from the Australian Rugby Union that it should take place in one country it actually took place across five! As Wyatt (1996) notes this decision to hold the competition in five countries with four different legal systems, three different currencies and two different languages 'was a recipe for disaster' (p. 57). The fact that the competition was taking place in Europe, with Romania and Italy joining the five nations as the other countries from this continent taking part, saw a marked increase in television viewing figures. There had also been a massive change in the broadcasting environment since 1987 with three dedicated sports channels now operating in Europe. This event, much more so than the first tournament, pointed towards the commercial potential of a world cup competition and made (some of) those involved in the game sit up and take notice of the potential economic gains to be made through the tournament. England's progression to the final of the competition attracted significant media attention at a time when many of its players were starting to become more and more recognized. Their captain, Will Carling, in particular, was a regular feature in a range of media and (as will be discussed in Chapter 4) became one of the first rugby players to be deemed a 'celebrity'. In the final the English were defeated by an Australian side, thereby ensuring that the trophy would remain in the southern hemisphere for at least another four years. The established order of the game was threatened when a poor Wales side lost to Western Samoa in the group stages although part of the reason for this was attributed to the loss of many leading Welshmen to rugby league (see Chapter 3).

South Africa had not taken part in the first two world cups due to its exclusion from the international sporting community on account of its apartheid regime. The decision to award the 1995 finals to South Africa, three years after its readmission into international rugby, concerned many for when the tournament was awarded to the nation (in 1993) it continued to be plagued by political violence (Black and Nauright, 1998; Carlin, 2008). Nelson Mandela's election as the first black president of the country in 1994 ensured that the tournament would be much more than just a sporting contest and would be used as an opportunity to present images to the rugby-playing world and beyond of a new South Africa (see especially, Carlin, 2008; Farquharson and Majoribanks, 2003). It is worth noting that it took the international football authorities 80 years to hold a world cup in Africa. Given that rugby was the one sport most connected with apartheid oppression this was a decision many were not comfortable with at the time but few could have predicted the seismic events that changes in the nation would bring and how the progress of the home team would ensure that this 'became the most significant trans-racial moment of celebration' (Black and Nauright, 1998: p. viii) since the 1994 all-race elections.

For many different reasons the 1995 event was a momentous occasion and put the sport of rugby in the news in a way that it had not witnessed before or since. Louis Luyt's, the President of the South Africa Rugby Football Union (SARFU), tactless comments that this was the first real world cup given South Africa's absence from the first two soured things somewhat but could not detract from the general positive images that surrounded the tournament. The sight of Nelson Mandela, wearing the Springboks shirt of the captain Francois Pieenar, presenting the trophy to the big Afrikaner was an image beamed around the world and remains the most viewed rugby-related image of all time. This will cement its place in people's memories even more as Carlin's (2008) book has been adapted into a Hollywood film directed by Clint Eastwood and starring Morgan Freeman as Mandela and Matt Damon as Pieenar. Released in December 2009 *Invictus* might do more to raise awareness of the sport in some markets than any number of IRB initiatives ever could.

Outside the momentous events in re-imagining a new South Africa, the Scotland captain Gavin Hastings set a new points scoring record in this tournament with a personal tally of 44 points when Scotland defeated the Ivory Coast 89-0 but this was surpassed by a point by the New Zealander Simon Culhane when his nation scored 145 points against Japan. While the performances of the Ivory Coast highlighted the lack of depth in rugby across the African continent, Japan have long been regarded as part of the second level of nations in world rugby and the leading country in Asia. The nature of such defeats led to questions about what was gained from such an exercise and offered a pertinent point of reflection on the challenges of developing a truly international sporting competition. By the time the next world cup took place the sport would have been openly professional for four years and things would never be the same again.

World Cups in the professional era

So after the drama and excitement of the 1995 finals the Paris Declaration of August that year witnessed the end of a century-old tradition and rugby union became a professional game. While an open game was an inevitable outcome of the formation of South Africa, New Zealand and Australia Rugby (SANZAR) and the media battle for control of the sport there continued to be much resistance, and some denial, to the fact that the game was now professional. Yet just because the game had now accepted professionalism this did not mean that the established order would be changed. Although it was clear that the increased commercialization of the sport would also mean that those leading the game should adopt a more international outlook, the narrow mindset and self-serving interests of many involved in its governance saw to it that the sport coughed and spluttered its way into professionalism.

Writing in 2008 the authors of the *Putting Rugby First* report noted that 'the IRB's commitment to internationalization is not consistent with its decisions on the location of its flagship event, the RWC – which has never been held outside a Foundation Union' (Spectrum Value Partners and Addleshaw Goddard, 2008: p. 6). Interestingly, and as noted previously, one of the key recommendations following the first world cup was that all future tournaments should be held solely in one country and that joint bids should be discouraged. The dominance of the foundation unions and the 'old boys network' is important to note here for the voting process across the years has seen unions encouraged to back a particular bid in exchange for being awarded matches. The first world cup of the openly professional era was hosted by Wales but matches also took place in England, France, Ireland and Scotland. The Millennium Stadium had been built at a cost of 114 million British pounds to stage the final of this event and resulted in massive debts for the Welsh Rugby Union (WRU) early into the new century. Their counterparts at the Football Association in England, whose difficulties in securing the redevelopment of Wembley Stadium meant that Cardiff staged FA Cup finals and football league play-off matches for a few years, saved the WRU in some ways as without this additional income the debt could have spiraled out of control.

In the 1999 rugby world cup just over a fifth of all matches actually took place in Wales and the two semi-finals were both played at Twickenham in England. Few were even aware that the world cup was going on in Scotland and miserable attendance figures and limited media attention left many feeling that the world cup had never actually taken place there. Poor scheduling of matches meant that the tournament often seemed to grind to a halt and the overall economic impact was much lower than widely claimed (Jones, 2001). Australia became the first nation to win the trophy for a second time as they further demonstrated their continued ascent as a sporting nation and an ability to adapt to the demands of the open era of rugby.

Despite the recommendations noted before about future world cups needing to be based solely in one country and some of the issues surrounding the promotion and marketing of the 1999 event, the

2003 tournament was scheduled to be staged in Australia and New Zealand but a dispute over 'clean stadiums', whereby there would be no conflicting advertisements or sponsorship agreements, meant that in the end the event only took place in Australia. Coming just three years after the country had hosted a very successful Olympic Games, and drawing upon the extensive marketing and management expertise of industry professionals, this event was markedly different to the previous world cup. This tournament was also significant for it represented the first, and to date only, victory for a team from a northern hemisphere nation. The planning and attention to detail of the hosts reflected the professional approach that had brought the nation to the forefront of sport management and development (Stewart et al., 2004). In a similar way, Clive Woodward's England was the epitome of professionalism and organizational excellence. Adapting strategies learnt from his successful business career Woodward was able to oversee a massive change to the structure and function of the national team (Dallaglio, 2007; Hill, 2006; Leonard, 2004; Woodward, 2004). The growing support structure implemented to achieve this reflected England's financial positioning and put them many years ahead of the majority of other nations in terms of their planning and preparation. With more stadiums now including floodlights, matches could also be scheduled to suit the needs of key international television markets though it must be noted that in this case it refers largely to the core nations, for in the really big television markets like the US rugby was not an attractive proposition. Following in the sizeable footsteps of Jonah Lomu, whose performances at the 1995 world cup catapulted him into the spotlight, in 2003 it was England's Jonny Wilkinson whose match-winning performance in the final ensured that his life would alter significantly (see Chapter 4).

France hosted the tournament in 2007 although matches also took place in Scotland and Wales. England had competed with France to stage the 2007 event but was comprehensively defeated when voting to decide on the hosts took place. This defeat provided a sharp rebuttal to the RFU who many felt were arrogant and somewhat condescending in their proposal where they put forward a template to drastically alter the structure of the finals. It seems that the lessons were learnt for their (successful) bid to host the 2015 tournament focused more on what the event would do for the wider international rugby community. In 2007 matches took place in ten cities across the country although the capital city of Paris staged most of the key games and saw by far the largest financial impact of all parts of the country (Hautboir and Charrier, 2009). South Africa defeated England in the final in a match-up that few would have predicted at the start of the tournament to become the second nation to win the trophy twice and also to ensure that it would return to the southern hemisphere for the fifth time in six attempts. Wales continued its cycle of losing to one of the small south sea island nations but this time it was Fiji who claimed a victory against them. Portugal competed in the finals for the first time and although they finished at the bottom of their group without managing a victory they put in some impressive performances and were not disgraced.

World rugby core and periphery: The next three world cups

The opportunity to expand the global positioning of the game and develop the sport internationally was a key discussion point in the months leading up to deciding where to stage the 2011 World Cup. Many had expected those governing the game to support their words with actions and award the finals to Japan as evidence of a developing internationalization agenda. Yet when it came to making the decision New Zealand was awarded the competition and so would host the event for the second time. Authors of the *Putting Rugby First* report have critically evaluated the role of the IRB in failing to develop the game in a global context noting that awarding the 2011 tournament to Japan would have meant staging the tournament in a country with a much larger economy and 'would have provided a springboard to the fast-growing Asian economies' (Spectrum Value Partners and Addleshaw Goddard, 2008: p. 6). The football world cup had been co-hosted by Japan in 2002 and the nation was a central part of an identified strategy by numerous sports leagues and franchises to break into and/or further capitalize on the economic potential of the Asian market (Giulianotti and Robertson, 2009; Klein, 2006). Yet parochialism seemed to loom large again in the rugby world as the voting dictated that New Zealand would host the event.

In the IRB the eight foundation unions each have two votes while there are four votes allotted to (selected) 'Tier 2' nations. The remaining members of the IRB share just six votes between them that are distributed to the continental representative bodies. For many commentators the decision not to award the 2011 competition to Japan came as no surprise as parochialism and self-serving governance had been a constant during the history of the game. The Asianization of rugby represents an integral part of any real push to develop the game globally and take the sport outside its narrow core. Rugby has a very different place in Japan where the high school and university system supports teams run by major corporations and the sport is an important tool in promoting traditional notions of masculinity (Light, 2000). Major corporations who support and field rugby teams, see the game as an important part of their identity. Kobe Steel were the first corporate rugby team, formed in 1945, and were also the first to field foreign players when two Oxford graduates played there in 1978 (Sakata, 2004). The impact of foreign players both within the companies and the national team represents a somewhat problematic issue in relation to promoting and reinforcing identities (Light, Hirai and Ebishima, 2008; Sakata, 2004) and is a subject I will return to in subsequent chapters.

In 2009 the IRB announced the hosts for the 2015 and 2019 world cup competitions. The decision to announce both hosts at the same time and the late changes regarding financial guarantees attracted further controversy. It is also important to note that the decisions on where to stage the 2015 and 2019 competitions took place amidst a global economic crisis and stated concerns surrounding predicted financial losses for the 2011 event. One newspaper likened the RFU's new attitude of doing anything they could do to help in such times as a throwback to the spirit of 1948 when London stepped in to host the Olympic Games following the ravages of World War II.

In 2019 the first world cup to take place in Asia will see Japan at the centre of the rugby world. This may in the contemporary language of rugby governance be seen as evidence of 'reaching out' but it is also a sensible financial decision for few of the nations at the core of international rugby have anything close to the economic power of Japan. It also represented an astute political move as the game continued to actively try and secure its seat at the Olympic table. When Japan was awarded the 2019 tournament the President of the Japan Rugby Football Union (JRFU), Yoshiro Mori, noted that 'our goal – the globalization of rugby – is getting closer to reality'. While some of this chapter is critical of the IRB's commitment to internationalization it is worth noting that it took the Olympic Games and the football world more than 70 years to stage their flagship events in Asia. In all cases Japan was a central player and for the rugby world Japan is important as it is the longtime highest ranked nation in Asia and a place where the game is well established (Light, Hirai and Ebishima, 2008).

As predicted the 2015 event will return to England, the self-styled 'home' of the game, given that the RFU promised a significant financial return on the competition. This was important because somewhere in the region of 95 per cent of the IRB's income comes from the world cup. In their continued talk of developing a truly global game this makes the decision to award the 2011 finals to a small nation with a limited economy all the more strange particularly when considered alongside their stated goal to 'maximise the profile, profitability and value of Rugby World Cup' (IRB, 2004: p. 4).

Utilizing the many excellent football stadia in England this meant that the infrastructure was already in place for the RFU's bid. This was an important factor given the ongoing concern regarding the escalating costs of the London 2012 Olympic Games where initial estimates were later corrected to be billions of pounds below what the real cost will be. Strangely, but not to those with any awareness of the politics prevalent in the sport, matches in the 2015 event may also be staged at the Millennium Stadium in Cardiff. Elsewhere I have commented on this issue of viewing *EnglandandWales* as one place (Harris, 2008) in relation to the promotion of Welshness and identifying the Principality as a nation in its own right but economic factors seem to over-ride any concerns in this respect. A debate continues as to whether the Millennium Stadium can be used as part of an English world cup and questions remain as to whether Wales should be allowed to play their matches there during the competition.

As a reflection on the changing place of the game, or as just a concerted attempt to ensure they were awarded the competition, New Zealand pushed for holding the 2011 event on the basis that after that the competition would become too big an event for them to stage. While this represented an astute political move it also means that the country has effectively ruled itself out of hosting another tournament in the foreseeable future. Ireland, Scotland or Wales would not seem to have the infrastructure or support to host a tournament on their own. Italy, given their many large football stadia and increased standing in the union game, must surely be a contender to host a world cup in the 2020s. It would seem likely that South Africa would also get to host another world cup and both of these nations bid to host the 2015 event. But once these two nations have hosted a tournament where can the rugby world cup go then?

Undoubtedly, as with many other sports, the US holds significant appeal to those interested in developing the economic aspects of the sport. Yet even though many may point to the success of the 1994 football world cup finals in the country, a decision based solely on finances rather than football-related issues (Horton, 1995), rugby's positioning remains far below that of football (soccer) in the sporting landscape. Indeed the unquestionable dominance of another football code (American football) means that the majority of boys with the right physical attributes to play rugby are already playing another game and one that offers the promise of university scholarships and perhaps untold wealth if they were to make it all the way to the heights of the professional game. An event to clearly illustrate the gap between the two sports was when ESPN screened a US rugby international live for the first time when the US Eagles faced off against Canada in a world cup qualifier in July 2009. The sudden death of a former football player, Steve McNair, meant that the rugby match was moved to a different channel for the second-half coverage.

Ideologies of power, dominance and the exalted status of a narrow core are central to the whole history of the game. Romantic delineations that the sport is a game for all need to be taken with a pinch of salt for the game has always been governed and controlled by a very small group of men (Chandler and Nauright, 1996; Wyatt, 1996). Yet in reality rugby is no different to the vast majority of other sporting organizations governed by a small power elite where dominant ideologies of class, gender and nation are promoted and celebrated. Indeed given its relatively narrow reach it would probably be fair to surmise that the sport is even more insular than many other sporting organizations. I have already briefly touched on the importance of the nation and the hegemony of England, the home unions and issues of empire. Rugby's gendered positioning is a subject that will be revisited although the very fact that this is a book about professional rugby, men's rugby, clearly highlights that in many ways the game remains something of 'a male preserve' (Sheard and Dunning, 1973). That the sport is described as a gentleman's game, albeit one played by hooligans (Richards, 2007), adds further to this conceptualizing of rugby as the making of men (see especially, Nauright and Chandler, 1996).

When considering the significance of social class to the sport and the power dynamics involved in shaping the game then nothing illustrates this better than the relationship between rugby union and rugby league. The next chapter looks at what the open professionalization of rugby union did to the relationship between the two codes. Here, after providing an overview of some of the background to the changes in both games and the role of the media in this, I focus largely on Wales and Australia as two nations where the movement of league players into the union game was particularly significant.

3
Power Shifts: From League to Union

The great divide between league and union was often presented as a simplistic dichotomy of professionalism versus amateurism. This suited accounts that encompassed derogative descriptors of league and was applied in countries such as Wales and Australia to help explain periods of poor performances for the national XVs when they had lost many of their best players to the thirteen-man code. Yet in reality the differences and the divide were never as simple as this. As Tony Collins (1998, 2006) has detailed, many league players were given jobs by their clubs and had to supplement their income from the game with outside work. Few could earn enough just from the sport itself. Conversely, despite an expressed ideology of 'amateurism', a number of union players had always been well rewarded for their exploits on the field in the fifteen-man game. The Australian winger David Campese spent his winters playing for the Milan club in Italy long before the game went openly professional. In addition to his outstanding skills and outspoken personality, Campese was known for claiming to be the first millionaire rugby union player! Commentators had noted years before that his winters spent in Milan were not because of his love of spaghetti. There are numerous other cases of southern hemisphere players 'wintering' in Italy. At times it was the wealthy men that bankrolled clubs who arranged for jobs for players within their companies. This practice stretched across continents, for the role of major corporations in Japanese rugby saw a number of top players move there to represent company teams (see I. Williams, 1991). The former England international Mike Catt notes how the owner of Bath RFC found him a job in the days of amateurism and that numerous other players worked for his range of companies (Catt, 2007). Later on the prevalence of Development Officer posts by clubs and national unions provided a means to offer players a job, a sponsored car and great flexibility in their work commitments but still remain 'amateur'. While this is not to say that (in some cases) players had to work hard and indeed may have had to sometimes earn their jobs on merit, what the above clearly highlights is how there were numerous ways around the issue of payment for playing the game and that the area was much more complex than simplistic delineations of amateurism versus professionalism claim.

One hundred years after rugby's great split (see Collins, 1998) the open professionalization of rugby union saw the fall of the game's Berlin Wall (Williams et al., 2005). To conceptualize this it is worth noting Friedman's (2007) observation that the fall of the Berlin Wall six years earlier was an important moment in the flattening of the world and the new age of globalization. Almost a hundred years earlier rugby's own 'Berlin Wall' was built because of the fear that control of the game would be wrest away and become controlled by the working classes. Collins (2009), a leading authority on rugby league, argues that while the open professionalization of rugby union in 1995 may have once again threatened the established order, unlike in the late nineteenth century this time 'the essential nature of the sport was not under threat' (p. 214). Despite the limited appeal of rugby union as a global sport, when compared to rugby league it is very much a more popular and wider reaching sport. The thirteen-man game is played in an even smaller number of nations than the union game and so the open professionalization of the latter was bound to have a marked impact on the former.

Some players made the switch from league to union once the latter had become openly professional; although as Collins (2006) notes despite fears of a player exodus 'a mere handful of league players switched to union' (p. 192). Top league players such as Wendell Sailor (Australia) and Jason Robinson (England) were tempted to test their skills in the fifteen-man game as rugby union sought to lure some of the most prolific try scorers from their rival code. For although the mid-1990s had witnessed seismic change in union, rugby league had also undergone significant alterations, again shaped by media forces. After being played as a sport in winter for more than a century, rugby league in England is now played in the summer months. Before looking at the cases of Australia and Wales I firstly look at how the media were influential in reshaping the wider rugby landscape and the relationship between the two codes.

Mediascapes and the rugby wars

The media play a central role in sport today. Scholars have highlighted the symbiotic relationship between the two, the power of the media in changing established traditions, and the ways in which contemporary sport relies on the media to finance it (e.g. Boyle and Haynes, 2000; Raney and Bryant, 2006). Horton (1996: p. 6) notes how mediascapes represent 'the single most important dimension of the cultural flow towards globalisation' for sport while Hutchins (1998), as discussed in the previous chapter, has pointed to the pivotal role of the media in the development of the rugby world cup.

As part of the SANZAR triumvirate, together with New Zealand and South Africa, Australia were the key drivers in the open professionalization of rugby. Of course it was an Australian, Rupert Murdoch, who did more than anyone to alter the landscape of the rugby world as a whole vexing considerable power over both codes. Andrews (2004) provides a good overview of the work of News Corporation and Murdoch's use of sport as a 'battering ram' for entry into new markets throughout the world. Murdoch's experience in the UK where securing the rights to English Premier League football was a key step in developing his business interests in that part of the world emphasized the importance of sport in the process of shaping News Corporation into 'a truly global media power' (Andrews, 2004: p. 12). Horsman (1997) shows how Murdoch's satellite television interests moved from an organization haemorrhaging money to the world's most profitable media channel television company. The centrality of football to this development is clear and is the focus of a separate section of Horsman's text. Rugby, despite being a part of this strategy of using sport as a 'battering ram', is not mentioned hence reflecting its marginal status when compared to football.

It was a battle for control of the two rugby codes that ultimately reshaped the landscape and relations between the sports. News Corporation's success in purchasing monopoly rights to rugby league has been well documented elsewhere (e.g. Collins, 2006; Colman, 1996). The increased salaries now on offer in rugby league unsettled many of those involved in the union game who foresaw losing many more players to the thirteen-man code. Alongside this, developments in rugby union pushed the sport to the point where it had to change despite the obvious reluctance of many of those involved in its governance. Fitzsimons (1996) suggests that the formation of SANZAR and the deal that was later agreed with News Corporation was motivated by the threat of a cross-continental rugby league competition attracting many of the top union players. Another challenge arrived in the shape of the World Rugby Corporation, which aimed to create 30 rugby union franchises worldwide. By August 1995 the organization had claimed the signatures of more than 400 of the world's top players with the promise of annual six figure salaries for many. Interestingly this proposal included the possibility of franchises in the US and Japan but ultimately the power remained with the national unions and they appealed to the players' sense of national identity and heritage emphasizing the importance of the jersey and their commitment to their nation (Fitzsimons, 1996; Hutchins, 1996). The battle for control of the union game resulted in a massive influx of money as the sport moved into the open era of professionalism. Nicholls (2006: p. 112) suggests that

> [t]he deal not only 'saved' rugby from the vultures of rugby league but it changed the look of international rugby forever. In the southern hemisphere, it meant that the concept of the traditional tour would become as rare as hen's teeth and that the top players would become commercial servants to the almighty television dollar.

So while it is clear that the developments outlined above had a massive impact upon the very heart of both rugby codes, it also led to numerous suggestions that the two games would have to merge and form a hybrid game. In the early years of open professionalism in union, and the beginnings of summer rugby in Super League, the idea of year-round rugby players who could ply their trade in both codes was often put forward. As the physical demands of the game and the many differences between the two sports became more apparent this idea disappeared pretty quickly. The predictions of witnessing a hybrid game stemmed in part from the changes to the actual playing of the union game that open professionalism fostered. Bigger and faster men meant that there was less space on the field of play and in many ways it seemed to more closely resemble rugby league. This was perhaps influenced in part by the increasing influence of former rugby league men in the coaching structures of many union teams (see also, Chapter 6). What we have certainly seen with their arrival is much improved defensive structures in the union game. At times this has caused great concern for in contemporary times sport also needs to 'entertain' and complaints about the lack of tries scored in matches was commonplace. Certainly in the early years of open professionalism far less attention appeared to be afforded to attacking skills as teams focused primarily on not losing matches and defensive stalemates were settled through the boots of highly proficient goal kickers. This again was a logical outcome of professionalism for now results mattered more and as paid employees of clubs the players lost, what the former England coach Dick Greenwood referred to as, the amateurs inalienable right to play like a pillock.

Some former rugby union players were tempted back from league in a journey that many would never have conceived possible when they made the decision to change codes. Theirs were to be the first return journeys over rugby's Berlin Wall for prior to the professionalization of rugby union once they had 'defected' to rugby league they were persona non grata and banned for life from any involvement with the union code. Alan Tait represented Scotland in rugby union before embarking upon a successful career with Widnes RL and becoming a Great Britain international in the thirteen-man code. He became the first former professional to return to the Scottish national team when he returned to union in 1997. Martin Offiah played for Rosslyn Park and was earmarked by some as a future England international but he moved to rugby league before this was to become a possibility when he joined Widnes in 1989. Offiah was arguably one of the best union converts to have 'gone North' and he scored a number of tries for Widnes before moving to Wigan for a record transfer fee. Towards the end of his career Offiah played a few games for Wasps but struggled to adjust back to his first game unlike Tait who was selected to tour with the British and Irish Lions during the year he moved back to union (see also, Chapter 8). Yet while all nations were affected in some ways by the loss of their leading players to rugby league it was a particularly pertinent issue in Wales and Australia. In the next section I touch on the history of the migration of Welsh union players to the north of England and then look at their migration out of England when they were able to return to their first sport. While much of the movement in Australia occurred within its national boundaries I focus on the Australian case as a means of identifying contemporary issues and controversies that are pertinent when considering the relationship between the two codes today.

The road to Wigan pier ... and back again

In what was a key marker in developing the academic focus on labour migration in sport, Bale and Maguire's (1994) edited collection provided an array of examples detailing the movement of athletic talent across the globe. Within this Gareth Williams presented a historical account of the migration of Welsh union players to rugby league noting that it 'has been a source of magnetic attraction' (G. Williams, 1994: p. 26). Focusing on the migration of players from 1918 through the early 1990s, Williams analysed the movement of players from Wales within and around an examination of the changing social and economic landscape of the country. He noted that in the period from 1895 to 1990, of the 227 international rugby union players from the home unions (England, Ireland, Scotland and Wales) who changed codes, 156 of them were from Wales (G. Williams, 1994). This visibly shows how rugby union in Wales was more affected by the movement of its international representatives to rugby league than any of the other home unions. It is also important to note that this figure only refers to those who had already been capped at the full international level and many more players took the same road before they had the chance to represent the national team.

G. Williams (1994) estimated that in total some 2000 Welsh rugby players went 'north' in the period, with close to 900 moving between 1919 and 1939, although the more recent work of Collins (2006) suggests that this figure is an over-estimation and that less than half that amount actually made the transition. Periods of economic prosperity and economic decline in Wales have often mirrored the position of the national rugby team. At times of serious economic hardship such as between the two world wars, and in the Thatcherite period of the 1980s, a number of players left the game in Wales for the financial rewards on offer in league. Of course it was not just during such periods that players took the road north. Throughout the history of the game many Welshmen had left their homes in the Principality to seek a better life in the north of England. As Collins (2006: p. 54) has noted:

> Rugby league's appeal to Welsh rugby union players was simple. It offered them the opportunity to benefit financially from their footballing skills. Many were given jobs on a club's ground staff or with companies connected to club directors. For others, clubs guaranteed to make up a minimum wage if the job that was found for the player did not pay an adequate sum. Some were given the tenancy of a pub.

G. Williams (1994) argues that Wales was far more susceptible to losing its players to the league game because of the social positioning of the union game in the Principality. In England the sport had been built around a code of amateurism nurtured by a social elite (Collins, 2009) but in Wales it grew alongside an industrialization of the southern valleys where mass immigration and economic growth were defining features (Holt, 1989). Because of the massive influx of migrants to the south Wales coalfields during the industrial revolution, the population of the country increased markedly and this dramatically changed the social and cultural landscape. Rugby union became the national game of Wales not because of any particular cultural affinity but because of the close geographical proximity of south Wales to the west of England (G. Williams, 1991). If it was the industrial revolution and the rapid urbanization of south Wales that partly explains why the sport became an integral part of the sporting landscape in the Principality, then the open professionalization and increased internationalization of the game needs to be considered in terms of how it both challenged and reinforced the place of the sport in contemporary Wales.

Although the 'incipient professionalization' of the sport was a focus of Dunning and Sheard's (1979) text on the development of rugby football and had been the subject of various workshops/ committees in the rugby world for some time, the sport was ill prepared to cope with the change to professionalism. It was in some ways forced upon those who governed the game and many of those who were in positions of power saw professionalism as a real threat to their hegemony and status. Writing more broadly about the concept of hegemony, Williams (1977) has noted that the power of this hegemony is never absolute and at any time alternative or even directionally opposite politics are at play. This political wrangling has perhaps defined the game more than anything else in the period since 1995.

In Wales talk centred on the potential return of recent league converts such as Scott Quinnell, Dai Young and Scott Gibbs. The biggest star of all, and the man who was the focus of most newspaper stories though was Jonathan Davies. Davies, who had represented the Wales Rugby Union team many times in the revered number ten shirt, had moved to rugby league in 1989. His decision was influenced in large part by his frustration at the incompetence and petty bureaucracy of those involved in the governance of the game. As he noted of his request to address the Annual General Meeting of the WRU, not long before he finally decided to leave for Widnes, 'I couldn't have been treated with more contempt if I'd suggested digging up the National Stadium and planting potatoes' (Davies, 1989: p. 136).

Despite his small stature and the many predictions that he would fail, Davies proved a big success in the thirteen-man code, where he won team and individual trophies, captained a resurgent Welsh team to a European title and represented Great Britain. If there was one player who could symbolically highlight the shift in the relationship between union and league then Davies was the biggest catch of all. In November 1995 Davies moved from Warrington RL to Cardiff RFC in a deal aided by the WRU. There was some resentment from other clubs that the WRU had helped Cardiff with the transfer and this was a theme to reoccur in both Welsh and English rugby when a player was signed from rugby league. Many of his new teammates at Cardiff also seemed less than pleased with the return of the player and it appeared in some matches as if Davies was being deliberately ignored and starved of the ball. Yet despite being past his best, having returned home after reaching his peak in the thirteen-man code, Davies found himself recalled by the Welsh selectors after an eight-year absence.

While at Warrington RL, Davies had played alongside a teenager born in Oldham (Lancashire), who would himself one day also make the journey to play in Wales. This man, Iestyn Harris, developed into one of the top rugby league players in the country and in 1998 was awarded the 'Man of Steel' trophy, the biggest individual honour in the game. As his Christian name indicates Harris, who was born and raised in the heartland of rugby league, is of Welsh ancestry. His grandfather, Norman Harris, had played for Newbridge but was one of the many players tempted to rugby league in the 1940s. Like many other Welshmen who had made the move to the league game he settled in the north of England after his playing career had finished.

Cardiff RFC and the WRU secured the services of Harris against stiff competition from the RFU in England who wanted Harris to wear the red rose. Harris, who was proud of his Welsh roots, had captained the Wales Rugby League team and notes in his autobiography, '[m]y father and grandfather ensured the young Iestyn Harris had the three feathers in his heart from day one' (Harris, 2005: p. 49). His was a particularly significant signing not just because of his exceptional skills and status as one of the biggest talents in the thirteen-man game but because he was the first signing made by Wales of someone born and raised in rugby league. This transfer symbolized something of a power shift in the relationship between (Welsh) rugby union and rugby league. Dunning and Sheard (2005) noted that since rugby union went openly professional no high-profile union player had made the switch to rugby league yet it should be noted that many league converts have returned to the thirteen-man game having failed to make the impact in the fifteen-man code that they were expected to. This is something that has received a great deal of media attention in Australia and is a subject that I will return to shortly.

From 1995 some players had experimented with 'dual contracts' that allowed them to play both sports although the differences in the two games and the physical demands of year-round rugby meant that such experiments were short-lived. Although historically rugby league was often positioned negatively, and all Welsh union players who made the move were viewed as mercenaries, the reality was that many of the players who 'went North' had to supplement their income from playing the game with other work (Collins, 2006). It is also important to note that throughout the history of the amateur game many rugby union players remained in Wales because they were given jobs to enable them to stay.

Ironically in light of the 'Grannygate' affair (discussed in Chapter 7) it was the nationality of his grandfather that was highlighted in many newspapers as the reason for Iestyn's eligibility to represent Wales. Shortly after his transfer to Cardiff, Harris, despite never having played the game before, scored 31 points in his first full match against

Glasgow. This of course created significant hype and celebration in Wales with newspaper headlines such as 'Iestyn fever hits home' and 'Harris soaring to his destiny' proclaiming the arrival of 'The Great Redeemer (Mark II)' (Harris, 2006). The symbolic importance attached to Harris was also framed in a discourse that hinted how this was something of a payback to rugby league for all of the players they had tempted out of Wales for more than one hundred years. As an article in *The Observer* (October 28, 2001) newspaper noted:

> Not so long ago Welsh rugby would lose their favourite sons to rugby league and weep. Now a one-man mission from Leeds has reversed the trend and put a smile back on the face of the land of his forefathers. Iestyn Harris has arrived big time.

Harris was selected for his international debut against Argentina when he had played a sum total of two hundred minutes of rugby union in his life. Harris himself later reflected that his selection was motivated by external factors and was an attempt to increase ticket sales to the match (Harris, 2005). Somewhat predictably the player looked out of his depth and struggled to adjust to his new sport in the most unforgiving arena of international test-match rugby. His transfer, part-funded by the WRU, remained a contentious issue as many Welsh clubs struggled to survive in the professional game. While Harris became a fixture in the Welsh squad and appeared at the 2003 world cup finals within a short time he had returned to rugby league having not made the impact that was expected of him. His story is similar to that of a number of rugby league players on the other side of the world, and it is to the relationship between the two codes in Australia that I now turn.

The failed experiment

Lote Tuqiri's dismissal by the Australian Rugby Union (ARU) in the summer of 2009 highlighted what the national press identified as the failed experiment of league players in the union game. Tuqiri, the Fijian born winger, had previously played rugby league and was without doubt one of the most successful converts to the union game having represented Australia more than 60 times and scoring a try in the 2003 world cup final against England. Despite being a huge success on the field the player had various off-the-field issues with those governing the game and for some his departure was inevitable and more of a case of 'when' rather than 'if'.

Other high-profile league players who had been recruited to the union game had also left the sport in somewhat controversial circumstances. Wendell Sailor was banned from rugby union for two years when he tested positive for cocaine in 2006. Like Tuqiri, Sailor was a winger who had adapted well to the union game and achieved international honours in both codes of the sport. He proved himself to be a good international rugby union player, just like fellow cross-code convert Mat Rogers who moved back to league complaining about the complexities of the union game. Now playing for the Gold Coast Titans, Rogers is firmly established back in the thirteen-man code. Timana Tahu, who had once described rugby union as boring and noted how he wanted to play a sport where he would touch the ball more than once a game, changed his mind about the union game soon after and signed a lucrative deal with the ARU in 2007. Two years later he sought to be released from his contract with the ARU and signed a contract with his old league club Parramatta Eels for the 2010 season. For the 2009–10 season Ryan Cross remains the only high-profile league convert featuring in the Wallabies squad. A member of the Western Force squad, Cross was a junior international in the fifteen-man code before moving to rugby league as a teenager.

Australia provides another interesting case to look at because while rugby union is the national sport of Wales, the game is far less to the fore in Australia where rugby league and Australian Rules Football (Aussie Rules) enjoy an altogether more prominent and exalted position in the social and cultural landscape. Yet despite this, and as noted in the previous chapter, Australia won the second ever rugby union world cup competition and were the first nation to win the trophy twice when they repeated their success of 1991 eight years later. The fact that they had been able to win the trophy in 1991 despite losing players to the rival rugby code highlights the emerging talent identification and development system that was to make the nation the envy of much of the sporting world (Stewart et al., 2004). The impact of league on the union game could be seen by the fact that someone like Wally Lewis, widely regarded as one of the best ever rugby league players, was a schoolboy captain of the Australian national team in the union game. Collins (2006) has noted just how far advanced the

Australian league players like Lewis were compared to their English counterparts in the 1980s and how the sport was much more outward looking in its development in the land of the 'Kangaroos'. Horton (2009) notes how the two rugby codes in Australia remained ardent rivals based on an ideology of amateurism versus professionalism but accentuated through social class, education and occupation.

The importance of rugby league and of Aussie Rules in certain parts of the country continues to have a marked effect on the union game in Australia. As outlined earlier in the chapter both rugby codes saw seismic change as a result of media-led developments. There was much resistance to some of the changes in league where protests expressed local resistance to the commercialization of their sport and became a force for a patriotic anti-global Australian nationalism (Brawley, 2009; Grainger and Andrews, 2005). In addition to the relationship between the two rugby codes the Australian league international Karmichael Hunt is going to take the inter-code movement one stage further. Having signed with Top 14 team Biarritz in France to test his skills in the union game, Hunt has also signed a contract to play for Gold Coast in the Australian Football League for 2011 and he could become the first player in the professional era to play at the top level in all three sports.

In addition to the number of players who switched codes there are also other examples of players who not only changed rugby codes but also switched nations to further their careers in a different code. Craig Gower had played rugby league for the Australian national team. Having had a number of run-ins with the rugby league authorities in his home nation, Gower switched to the union game joining Bayonne in France and now represents Italy on the basis of having an Italian grandfather. Among his teammates for the Italian national team is fellow Australian Luke McLean who also qualifies through the 'Granny rule' (see Chapter 7).

The rugby world and the wider worlds of rugby

For those looking to return from rugby league in the professional age they did not have to return to their home country. For Welsh converts to rugby league the road from the north of England did not only lead to Cardiff. The open professionalization of the sport meant that players suddenly had a wide range of options to consider and could ply their trade as a rugby player in either code and in a number of different countries. Scott Quinnell left Wigan RL to join Richmond RFC on the outskirts of London and Adrian Hadley moved from Widnes RL to join Sale RFC just outside Manchester. So although for a century the rugby league clubs were blamed for many of the problems besetting the union game in Wales now many different roads in and out of the country presented new challenges to those involved in the governance of the game.

If I had returned to the Brewery Field in Bridgend in 2009 where many of my formative rugby experiences were shaped, I could have watched a game of rugby league as the Celtic Crusaders became the latest attempt to develop the thirteen-man code in south Wales. As with previous attempts to do this financial difficulties arose early on and the team finished bottom of the league. Some embarrassing revelations concerning visa issues also surfaced and six Australian players employed by the club were ordered to leave the country in the summer of 2009. At the end of the season Iestyn Harris was announced as assistant coach to the team thus making the journey to work in Wales for the second time in his rugby career. Yet unlike the hype and fanfare that surrounded his arrival in the Principality in 2001 this second stint attracted minimal media attention thus reflecting the marginal place of rugby league in Wales.

Although rugby union's failure to embrace globalization forms a key part of this text the fact that it has a wider reach and appeal than rugby league meant it was able to attract some of the best league players into the union game. Rugby league is played in an even smaller number of nations than the union game and fewer nations can realistically expect to be competitive in a world cup competition. Indeed as a professional sport of many years' standing the thirteen-man game has had a world cup competition more than 30 years longer than their union counterparts but it is clear that the fifteen-man version has overtaken the event of their league counterparts. It is interesting to note that the two codes face similar issues in terms of developing the sport and addressing the marginal place of the Fijian, Tongan and Samoan teams remains as much an issue in league as it does in union. It is obvious that these countries need the leading nations in their respective sports to make visits there and for those involved in the international governance of both codes to ensure that greater funds are made available.

With increased money and a greater visibility in the media, whatever the sphere, leads to wider recognition and the promise of greater rewards. Clubs and national governing bodies in the two codes could compete with each other with the salaries offered for playing the game but as the sports became more prominent in the media, athletes could now hope to capitalize on increased commercial opportunities outside the game. For the increased media exposure given to aspects of professional sport, and the investments made by companies such as News Corporation, players saw greater opportunities for developing their profile in the wider arena. The next chapter considers this increased exposure and status with a focus on the rugby player as celebrity.

4
The Rugby Player as Celebrity

On 2 December 2008 the *Daily Mail* newspaper considered it newsworthy that Wasps and England outside-half Danny Cipriani had taken his girlfriend out for a kebab. Described by the newspaper as 'the meal of choice for football fans and drunken lads out on the town', Cipriani's choice of food was deemed a national news story. Of course he is not the only 'celebrity' whose every move is logged and analysed. The 'celebrity' has become a defining feature of our times which in addition to a long-standing historical preoccupation with being famous is now also about celebrities becoming products themselves (Cashmore, 2006). Indeed it was the fact that Cipriani was dating the model/actress Kelly Brook that catapulted him into the sphere of 'celebrity' and increased his visibility in other areas of popular culture. Brook herself represents a conspicuous figure in the age of celebrity having previously dated, and been engaged to, actors Jason Statham and Billy Zane respectively. Both these relationships became a staple feature of newspaper gossip columns and magazine spreads. Such spaces have remained the preserve of actors and musicians for many years but not really the place where a rugby player was likely to appear. In this chapter I look at the place of celebrity in contemporary society, the increased visibility of the sporting celebrity and finally at the small number of rugby players who move beyond the sports pages and into the wider celebrity sphere.

The rise of the celebrity

The contemporary celebrity will usually have emerged from the sports or entertainment industries; they will be highly visible through the media; and their private lives will attract greater public interest than their professional lives.

(Turner, 2004: p. 3)

The ubiquitous celebrity has become a defining feature of the media-saturated postmodern age. Rojek (2001) has suggested that the secular culture of celebrity has emerged as one of the replacement strategies promoting orders of meaning and solidarity as organized religion has declined. Of course sport has also often been positioned as a kind of religion given that they have similar characteristics and produce similar experiences (e.g. Higgs, 1995; Hoffman, 1992). While it is beyond the scope of this chapter to dwell on this subject too much it is worth noting that both involve communal gatherings at important sites, they each have rituals and heroic accomplishments are celebrated. When considered in this context it comes as no surprise that sport stars tend to feature more and more within celebrity-focused magazines and on various Internet sites.

Turner (2004) has written of the para-social relationship between consumers and celebrities. This refers to the fact that relations of intimacy are constructed through the media rather than face-to-face meetings. Many people feel a connection with a particular celebrity despite the fact that they may never have actually met them. Increasingly it could well be that these connections become more important at a time when family and community relations may be less central to our identities. Cashmore (2006: p. 66) notes that celebrity culture is 'guided by the logic of consumerism' but also recognizes that consumers of celebrity are not passive dupes but have become willing accomplices in the enterprise. In locating the positioning of celebrities, Rojek (2001: p. 52) suggests that they offer 'powerful affirmations of belonging, recognition and meaning'. Redmond and Holmes (2007) note how the term 'celebrity' is now often used in a derogatory way to reflect the ways in which the term has become impoverished through the decline in talent, merit and achievement. What is clear is that in the late twentieth century, during the period when rugby became openly professional, we witnessed a shift of emphasis 'from achievement-based fame to media-driven renown' (Cashmore, 2006: p. 7). Yet even though there is much contention about what constitutes fame, and how it is now possible to be famous for being famous without demonstrating any discernible talent, the celebrity athletes remain somewhat different. The sports star occupies an important position for although their images and identities may be manipulated their skills as an athlete are laid bare and sport is 'one of the few areas of public life that is truly meritocratic' (Giles, 2000: p. 107). Before looking at the ways in which the rugby world has also entered the celebrity stakes I begin by looking more broadly at the emergence of the sporting celebrity.

The sporting celebrity

In recent years we have witnessed a marked interest from academics in the sporting celebrity (e.g. Andrews and Jackson, 2001; Smart, 2005; Whannel, 2002). Andrews and Jackson's (2001) edited collection on the cultural politics of sporting celebrity led the way here and provided a detailed insight into the ways in which the emergence of celebrity figures changed from being 'a haphazard and arbitrary voyage of discovery' (p. 4) to a much more proactive process focusing on cultivating celebrity. Featuring essays on athletes from sports such as football, tennis and basketball the contributors to this collection clearly outlined the dimensions of sports stardom and the positioning and significance of celebrity athletes in a range of cultural contexts. A few years later Smart (2005) provided another book-length treatise of the subject with in-depth analyses of David Beckham, Tiger Woods, Michael Jordan and Anna Kournikova to explain the commercialization and commodification of the sports star. The first three of the aforementioned were also the focus of chapters in Andrews and Jackson's (2001) collection reflecting the prominence of a select group of international sporting icons whose positioning and popular appeal transcend national boundaries (see also, Andrews, 2001; Cashmore, 2002; Halberstam, 1999). In between the two texts referred to above, Whannel (2002) authored a book on media sports stars looking at masculinities and moralities through examining the social and cultural significance of a range of high-profile athletes. What is noticeable about all these texts, and indeed the wider published literature on sporting celebrity that has become a staple feature of academic journals in the last decade, is the absence of rugby players. Rowe (1995) contends that before the 1970s there was nothing chic or fashionable about sports stars. Yet by the time that rugby union went openly professional sports stars were as chic and fashionable as pop stars and actors.

While only a select few athletes have become truly global sports celebrities, none of these have been rugby players. This reflects both the marginal position of the game in the USA, where the commercial power of celebrity is most prominent, and also the limited appeal of rugby in a global context. Yet rugby is no different than most other sports which have yet to claim their first truly global celebrity athlete. An athlete's celebrity stems not just from any discernible achievements in their chosen sport but through much broader cultural and economic processes. The context of sport is central here for, as is made clear within this text, rugby's failure to develop the game beyond a narrow collection of nations means that the sport has little social currency in a number of places beyond this group. Indeed, throughout the history of the sport leading players were for the most part largely local heroes and were not particularly popular beyond national boundaries.

Beyond local heroes

The amateur status of its players meant that even those leading lights of the international game were rooted in a sense of place and positioned very much as local heroes. The legendary 'voice of rugby' Bill McClaren's commentary on the British Broadcasting Corporation's (BBC) rugby coverage would state that they would be dancing in the streets of a particular town or village when one of their own scored a try, converted a successful kick or made a significant impact on a game. Here the local hero remained firmly entrenched in a sense of place. As John Daniell's (2009) honest, and at times amusing, *Confessions of a Rugby Mercenary* makes clear:

> Before the advent of professional rugby, a player played for the team in the town where he lived. You lived in that town because you worked or studied there, or simply because you were brought up there and it never occurred to you to move.
>
> (p. 7)

Yet the advent of open professionalism meant that players now moved because of rugby. I am not suggesting that before 1995 players did not move from their home or were not sometimes tempted to change clubs by the offer of a better job or some other perk. Rather, while this had occurred throughout the history of the game now in the professional age this movement became much more open and clearly directed by market forces. Rugby could now be a legitimate, and lucrative, profession in its own right so more players began to explore their options. Throughout the history of the amateur game elite rugby players earned their living in a variety of ways. All Black legend Colin Meads was a farmer; France's Jean-Pierre Rives worked as a sculptor; and the England prop Jason Leonard was a carpenter. Some of the most interesting accounts of how the game changed dramatically are provided by players whose careers transcended the periods of amateurism and open professionalism (e.g. Greenwood, 2005; Leonard, 2004; Thomas, 2007). For players such as these the shift was marked for they went from a world of having to try and fit their rugby around a day job (despite the presence of understanding employers) to one where they were full-time rugby players and their every need was catered for.

It is important to note that in contemporary times the term 'celebrity' is used somewhat loosely and often with little conceptual clarification. Yet rather than being a critique of the published works on the subject this does perhaps reflect the very essence of celebrity. As Cashmore (2006: p. 16) insightfully notes:

> Celebrity culture is a phenomenon that is simultaneously well known and little known. Many are fascinated by celebrities without actually understanding why they are fascinated. They know they are part of the process, yet not sure which part, nor how the process works. Everyone is aware of celebrity culture while remaining ignorant of when, where, and why it came into being. Maintaining this paradox is arguably the greatest triumph of celebrity culture.

In places where rugby is important, such as New Zealand, many of its leading rugby players may be considered celebrities. When New Zealand team members have a night on the town, in one of the nation's cities, they receive a great deal of attention. Yet these cases are usually structurally constrained within a particular geographic locatedness. Moreover unless something 'newsworthy' happens their celebrity remains firmly a matter of the local. In 2006 Tana Umaga, captain of the All Blacks, found himself the subject of much media attention for hitting teammate Chris Masoe with a handbag. This incident, which took place on a drunken evening out in a nightclub, was caught on the surveillance cameras of the club and such is the status of the sport in the country that the item in question was auctioned on the Trade Me website and sold for NZ $22,800 (*New Zealand Herald*, 5 June 2006). Generally though unless something particularly controversial happens rugby players fly under the radar of celebrity gossip columns and remain names only in the sports pages. Yet a select group of players transcend these boundaries. Because of who their girlfriends are Danny Cipriani and Gavin Henson receive a disproportionate amount of media attention when considered against the absence of more successful players in celebrity discourse.

The emergence of the rugby celebrity

Barry John of Cardiff and Wales was perhaps the first superstar of modern rugby. In his autobiography John (2000) talks of his friendship with the late George Best, a football player who struggled with the increased pressures that fame and celebrity status brought. It was following the Lions tour of New Zealand in 1971 that John's status and profiling soared. He recalled his shock at seeing himself pictured in the *New York Times* noting, 'I didn't think they had even heard of rugby in the United States' (p. 16). It was on returning from the 1971 Lions tour that he was referred to as 'the King'. Alongside contemporaries such as Gareth Edwards and Gerald Davies these men became famous throughout the rugby-playing world. Yet these players while feted and revered had jobs to return to once the game had finished. Indeed the challenge of being a celebrity playing an amateur sport was noted by John (2000: p. 17) who recalled:

> I would go straight from playing for Wales on a Saturday to mixing with the same members of the public who had been cheering me on thirty-six hours earlier. Inevitably they just wanted to talk about the game – I wanted to forget it.

John announced his early retirement from the game at the age of 27. This, he reflected, was influenced in part by the fact that a bank employee in Rhyl curtsied to him:

> Everyone applauded her actions, but that simply made matters worse as far as I was concerned. That moment made me realise that

I was alienated from ordinary people, that things had simply gone too far, that I was not like a normal human being anymore.

(John, 2000: p. 18)

Of course, as John (2000) himself acknowledges, his fame and the attention he received was a mere fraction of that afforded to Best. The worlds of rugby and football were far removed from each other in terms of their social and cultural positioning even then. Where a player such as John may have been regarded as one of the stars of rugby, in his case the George Best of the fifteen-man game, football enjoyed an altogether wider appeal and so its leading players were more recognizable. A player to follow Best into the Manchester United team and also wear the number seven shirt was David Beckham. While few would purport that he was comparable to the Irishman as a player, the massive changes of professional football during the early 1990s meant that Beckham achieved a status and celebrity far surpassing that of the man once described as 'the fifth Beatle'. I will return to the significance of Beckham shortly but first let's consider two other important figures in the rise of the rugby player as celebrity.

Jonah Lomu was without doubt the biggest name in rugby as the game went professional in 1995 and may well be described as the first star of the postmodern game. His remarkable impact as a 20-year old at the world cup finals in South Africa, including scoring four tries against England, catapulted him to international fame. Of course things did not just change overnight but the attention Lomu garnered saw something of a shift in rugby's traditional ways of thinking regarding the sizes and shapes of forwards and backs. The idea of a 260 lb man playing on the wing who could run the 100 metres in less than 11 seconds changed the status quo.

The two players named above were important figures in the gradual ascent of the rugby player as celebrity. Yet while John at the height of his fame actually had to sign on as unemployed and claim benefits at one stage, Lomu was able to capitalize on the attention he received as players could now legitimately be paid for playing the sport. He appeared in a Pizza Hut commercial shortly after the world cup and also signed a lucrative contact with Adidas (Grainger, Newman and Andrews, 2005). In the period between these two important players came Will Carling. Carling was appointed the captain of England at the age of 22 and led England during a very successful period where they reached a world cup final and won three Grand Slams. As a player whose career bridged the two eras he also represents an interesting figure in looking at how the game changed having established his own 'self-promotional company to capitalize on his fame' (Collins, 2009: p. 201) while still an amateur (see also, Carling and Heller, 1995). England's success in the early 1990s propelled the players to an increased degree of awareness and a greater level of attention than had been the case for many years. Certainly since rugby matches were first televised in colour during the 1970s England had struggled for many years. In addition to his status as captain of the national team Carling also moved outside of the sports pages through stories of a relationship with Diana, Princess of Wales. These revelations emerged as Carling split from his wife, Julia, and all of this drama was played out on the front pages of national newspapers hereby reflecting how famous Carling was. As a reflection of the commercial growth of rugby, on the cusp of professionalism, Carling employed the same agent as the England football captain Gary Lineker. While these two national team captains became well-known figures, their celebrity pales in comparison to that of a future England football captain who became arguably the biggest sports celebrity in the world.

Searching for the Beckham of rugby

Featuring on the cover of Whannel's (2002) text *Media Sport Stars* is David Beckham, one of the most famous sporting celebrities of the twenty-first century. Beckham is only really considered towards the end of the book but at the time this work was published his image, and name, appeared everywhere. Cashmore (2002) developed this analysis of Beckham further providing a book-length treatise of the athlete that explored the fascination with this person, the changing configurations of the sports industry and the transcending of the traditional boundaries between sport and entertainment (Cashmore and Parker, 2003). Social commentators such as Julie Burchill and Andrew Morton also considered the athlete worthy of book-length analysis (Burchill, 2001; Morton, 2000). There is no need to repeat the tale of the making of David Beckham here for his status and profiling is such that it needs little introduction. He is significant in the current discussion as a reference point in the media portrayals of rugby players.

For athletes in a range of sports Beckham became *the* marker to aspire to. Rugby was no exception to this as various players were positioned as the 'Beckham of rugby' by way of explaining their perceived status, looks and/or level of stardom. In the early years of the new millennium Jonny Wilkinson of Newcastle Falcons and England seemed to be the person most likely to fulfill this role. Born in 1979, Wilkinson was very much symbolic of the new breed of rugby players. As Huw Richards (2007: p. 267) noted:

> Two generations earlier, an academically competent Home Counties public schoolboy would have gravitated to Oxford or Cambridge and played three varsity matches. In the 1970s, he might have gone to Loughborough. Instead, Wilkinson went from school in Hampshire to a professional contract at Newcastle.

Collins (2009) describes Wilkinson as England's own 'modern incarnation of Tom Brown: talented, brave, modest, he was the embodiment of everything the English private school system hoped to produce' (p. 208). After the 2003 World Cup Wilkinson was said to have overtaken Jonah Lomu as the world's richest rugby player (Richards, 2007). Wilkinson had filmed a series of advertisements with Beckham for Adidas that proved popular. Yet unlike those involved with 'Brand Beckham', Wilkinson was a very private and reserved individual who was not comfortable in the limelight and if anything did much to consciously steer away from the 'celebrity circuit'. For in the age of 'celebrity' it is as much about being seen and heard, to be mingling with the right people and appearing at the perceived important events as it is about any discernible achievements. Whereas the quest for fame and attention seems to be a primary focus for many athletes, Wilkinson preferred to stand near the back of the bus in the open-top tour of London that celebrated England's world cup victory. An article on the BBC Sport website a day after England's defeat of Australia noted that 'while the likelihood of Wilkinson sauntering along to an Elton John party in a sarong is some way off, an increase in his commercial viability is almost inevitable' (BBC Sport, 2003).

After his match-winning drop goal against Australia in the 2003 World Cup final Wilkinson's profile rocketed to the extent that even

Beckham was kept off the front pages of newspapers. Numerous commercial opportunities presented themselves in the country that was the biggest and most financially lucrative rugby market and there were predictions of untold wealth and riches. Yet even among all the hype and fanfare there was at least some measured evaluation and commentators cautioned that England's hero was unlikely to reach the heights of Beckham or Tiger Woods because 'on a global level, rugby is not as big a sport as football or golf' (BBC Sport, 2003).

What is now often overlooked when commenting on the global visibility of David Beckham is that it was initially the greater fame and wealth of a celebrity girlfriend that first propelled Beckham beyond the sports pages. Similar terminology is visible in the 'celebrity' narratives of Danny Cipriani and Gavin Henson. I will look at the case of Cipriani later in this chapter; but initially I will consider the positioning of Gavin Henson as one of the first 'celebrity' rugby players of the professional age. As Ben Clayton and I have detailed elsewhere, because of his good looks and famous girlfriend (the singer Charlotte Church), Henson somewhat inevitably became labeled as 'the Beckham of rugby' or collectively the couple became positioned as 'the Beckhams of Wales' (Clayton and Harris, 2009; Harris and Clayton, 2007). Following his match-winning kick against England in 2005 Henson was ascribed almost overnight celebrity status. This somewhat unexpected victory was to be the first in a series of wins that would propel Wales to its first Grand Slam for almost 30 years.

Metrosexual rugby stars: The meaning of style

If as Rowe (1995) attests, sports stars became more fashionable and chic from the 1970s onwards then rugby players may have been viewed as the odd-men out in the sporting landscape. In stereotypical terms rugby was very much a game for hooligans and a sport for men of all shapes and sizes. It was a sport where after the game players were expected to drink copious quantities of beer and perhaps some aftershave for good measure. The following extract from the *Observer* (March 13, 2005) newspaper highlights how Henson's perceived difference made him an important figure in the game:

> Henson is an icon unlike any ever to grace a Welsh rugby pitch. He gels his hair, shaves his legs and wears gold boots. Twenty years

ago, when post-match celebrations meant drinking a skinful of beers and probably a bottle of aftershave, too, he would have been mocked. Now he is lionized – the first metrosexual rugby star.

As a group, rugby players rarely feature in and around discussions of the term metrosexual. Henson though, in the eyes of the media, represented something different and somewhat distinct within this particular subculture. One of his former coaches described to me how Henson applied fake tanning lotion before getting ready to go out onto the pitch. This of course was a marked contrast to some of the other players banging their heads against the walls and working themselves up into a frenzy in preparation for the match. The now iconic *Living with Lions* documentary following the 1997 tour to South Africa shows the different characters and pre-match routines of the game's leading players. While some, particularly in the forwards, needed to psyche themselves up for the battle ahead others would spend much of the pre-match warm-up throwing up in the toilet and nervously pacing the changing rooms not speaking to anyone else. With the prevalence of cauliflower ears and squashed noses many rugby players would be regarded as the antithesis of the metrosexual – and represent instead a throwback to more traditional masculine norms. Here the term 'retrosexual' has been employed to refer to a deliberate rejection of all things feminine and the simultaneously active pursuit of all things masculine (Clayton and Harris, 2009).

Yet in addition to these identifiable markers of difference Henson also serves as a visible symbol of the changes in the rugby world. Alongside open professionalism came the increased presence of support staff with leading clubs and national teams employing nutritionists, psychologists, masseurs, notational analysts and various other people to look after the players. Clive Woodward famously employed a vision coach during England's quest to win the world cup and also added a legal counsel to the 2003 World Cup party. Of course the consumption of vast quantities of alcohol did not just disappear from the game as Henson's (2005) own account of celebrating the 2005 Grand Slam attests. The former Leicester and England player Austin Healey (2006) also includes numerous tales of drunken escapades during his time in the sport (see also, Leonard, 2004; Thomas, 2007). More recently a member of the French national squad, Mathieu Bastareaud, created an international incident by claiming that the serious facial injuries he received were a result of being attacked by a group of five men while on tour with the national team in New Zealand. The story attracted much attention and led to official apologies from the Mayor of Wellington and the New Zealand Prime Minister on behalf of their country. It later transpired that the player had fallen while intoxicated and these revelations led to an official apology from the French Prime Minister to his New Zealand counterpart.

When critically assessing the rugby landscape it is clear that in addition to the mechanics of the game itself there are different off-the-field roles for forwards and backs (or 'fat boys' and 'girls' as they are sometimes differentiated in the language of the game). As this chapter has clearly highlighted, it is largely backline players who receive media attention and renown in relation to celebrity narratives. Few forwards would ever be labeled metrosexuals and only a small number ever enter into the realms of stardom and celebrity. As captain of the England team Lawrence Dallaglio was considered high profile enough to be the victim of a tabloid newspaper sting where he boasted about taking drugs to celebrate the Lions test series victory in South Africa. These allegations, published in the *News of the World*, led to Dallaglio being stripped of the England captaincy. The Bath prop forward Matt Stevens appeared on a celebrity edition of *The X Factor*, but garnered more attention for failing a drugs test in 2009 (for which he received a two-year ban from the sport) and admitting to a problem with recreational drug use. Of course one of the pitfalls of a 'celebrity' identity is that by virtue of being famous the individual was now fair game for media scrutiny. Narratives often take the shape of a rise and fall whereby the celebrity is perceived as someone needing to be brought down a peg or two. In recent years the sport of rugby has found itself appearing outside of the sports pages far too often leading to accusations that the sport is becoming more like football (see Chapter 9).

In the realms of stardom it is often the backs that are more likely to be afforded invites to film premieres and 'celebrity' television shows. In the celebrity age, although the very meaning of the term 'celebrity' remains a contested one (Cashmore, 2006), English rugby players could also be found on a variety of television shows. Matt Dawson followed in the footsteps of Bill Beaumont as a team captain on the popular television quiz show *A Question of Sport*. Dawson also went on to appear in *Strictly Come Dancing*. His old sparring partner, and for many seasons rival for the England number nine jersey, Austin Healey, also appeared on a later series of the show while Kyran Bracken competed in *Dancing on Ice*. Yet it is also important here not to view this as some compelling evidence of the ascent of the celebrity rugby player but should be viewed instead as more a reflection of the greater visibility of individuals from all spheres of public life. Indeed the average 'celebrity' show screened on television adopts a very tenuous interpretation of the term and among featured 'stars' of such programmes would be a former royal butler, an obscure member of a pop group who once made the charts and a reality television 'star' whose only discernible achievement was that they had appeared on another show.

Yet while some football players are recognized across the globe the vast majority of rugby players could walk down the main street of any number of cities in the world and go unnoticed. Rugby does not enjoy the same exalted status or global profile as football so it is important not to overstate the ascent of the rugby player as celebrity. In those places where rugby really does matter, it is hard for leading players and coaches to get away from the game. Certainly in Wales many have commented on the suffocating effect of the goldfish bowl existence of life in the capital city where seemingly everybody wants to talk rugby (e.g. Harris, 2005; John, 2000). Jonah Lomu would be recognized on the streets of Cardiff and Toulouse but may walk through many of the world's major cities in relative anonymity. As an article in *The Scotsman* (October 31, 2001) newspaper noted during the 2001 New Zealand tour of Britain and Ireland, 'Players as instantly recognizable as Tana Umaga walked up and down Princess Street with barely a glance in their direction.' So by and large it is only in a small number of places that many rugby players are recognizable due to their accomplishments on the field but some find themselves becoming the focus of greater attention through association.

Perfect ten: Outside-halves and scrummies

Outside halves feature prominently in the celebrity stakes. This is the glamour position on the field akin to the quarterback in American football or the star striker in the association game (Keating, 1993). We have already discussed Jonny Wilkinson's significance and profiling here although as detailed above Wilkinson was very much the reluctant star and did much to steer away from the celebrity circuit. Daniel Carter of the Crusaders and New Zealand is regarded by many as the greatest player in that position within the professional game. Voted the sexiest man in New Zealand, Carter was also the IRB's Player of the Year in 2005. He is an example of someone who has built a profile and reputation beyond the sport but is still celebrated for his skills as an athlete. Although sharing the same initials as Carter, Danny Cipriani represents a prime example of a more common narrative when athletes become part of the wider celebrity industry.

Danny Cipriani's relationship with Kelly Brook moved him into a world far removed from that of the 'average' English rugby player. An appearance at Milan fashion week in January 2009 sitting a couple of seats away from David Beckham, the quintessential postmodern sports celebrity, signified the rugby player's arrival in planet celebrity. Yet the visibility and exalted status brought about by being part of a celebrity coupling, and the developing of a profile beyond the game, is tempered by the fact that Cipriani still has to prove himself as a rugby player. At the start of the 2009–10 season Cipriani was not included in the elite England squad. Indeed, somewhat inevitably, his appearance within articles outside of the sports pages led to questions concerning his dedication and application. During the course of the 2009 Six Nations competition many English newspapers featured stories that his omission was due in part to his unpopularity among other players. This was given further currency when a training ground altercation with his Wasps teammate Josh Lewsey resulted in Cipriani being knocked to the floor. Gavin Henson was widely criticized in some quarters for his 'celebrity lifestyle' and narratives still talk of an 'unfulfilled talent'. Cipriani, like Henson, is now the focus of stories even when there is no story to tell. Perhaps this is the ultimate marker of celebrity. Or is it also about being 'famous by association'? This discourse of 'famous by association' usually works the other way whereby being linked with a prominent male athlete can propel a female into the news pages.

In line with the conspicuous consumption of football, and all that surrounds it, the last few years have seen the rise to media prominence of the WAG. These footballers' wives and girlfriends adorn the front pages of newspapers and magazines (Clayton and Harris, 2004). In needing to provide a reference point and find its equivalent, newspapers have recently begun to comment on the emergence of the scrummie. Here attention may be focused on television present-ers Gabby Logan and Kirsty Gallagher, equestrian rider Zara Phillips and the aforementioned Kelly Brook and Charlotte Church. Logan, Gallagher and Phillips are all daughters of international athletes and of course one is a member of the Royal family to boot. Unlike the stereotypical WAG, these women were all successful in their own right before meeting their partners. Logan (nee Yorath) and Gallagher both enjoy successful careers in television, despite some early misgiv-ings that their success was due to nepotism and/or was based largely on looks rather than broadcasting skills. As friends of many years' standing Gabby Logan, wife of the former Scotland international Kenny Logan, introduced Gallagher to Logan's former teammate Paul Sampson. In addition to being the granddaughter of the Queen, which meant that Phillips was already an ascribed celebrity, she is also an elite athlete in her own right having represented Great Britain and being named as the BBC's Sports Personality of the year in 2007. Yet even being a member of the Royal family does not make Phillips immune to criticism from the press. An article in the *Daily Mail* (March 25, 2009) suggested that she was turning into a 'Royal WAGness' noting:

> The only thing missing was a spray-on tan. Otherwise, from the oversize sunglasses to the exposed cleavage, ironed blonde hair and giant hoop earrings usually seen only on the ears of teenage single mothers pushing prams, Zara Phillips, as she watched fiance Mike Tindall play rugby for England, looked like an out and out WAG.

In many ways while the 'Beckham of rugby' tag will be applied in varying contexts, and in some ways serves the narrative of rugby becoming more like football, the scrummie serves an altogether dif-ferent role. Here class-based ideologies are at the forefront to signify that the scrummie is something markedly different to the WAG. For if WAGs are depicted as girls of limited intelligence and taste, trying desperately to be famous through association, then the scrummie is her antithesis. Even the broadsheet newspapers take an interest here with an article in *The Independent* (January 28, 2009) exploring the world of the scrummie noting that this is:

> the oval ball equivalent of the WAGs, that brand of designer-clad, champagne-quaffing women who, during the 2006 football

World Cup, accounted for nearly as many column inches as their other halves' sporting exploits with their drunken karaoke, exorbitant bar bills and shopping trips that would put a dent in third world debt.

The rise of the celebrity has led to a whole industry of people who are famous for being famous and seemingly have no accomplishments in any field. As Giles (2000) noted, sport stars are different here for their skills are judged in a meritocratic arena. Yet as Turner (2004) points out, although the process by which they first come to public attention may be different, to famous people in other spheres, sport stars are 'subject to the same mass mediated processes of celebritisation' (p. 19). As rugby has become more commercialized the media focus that surrounds the sport has increased.

At around the same time that Cipriani became a staple part of the celebrity news stories two other players found themselves appearing in newspaper headlines outside of the sports pages. Over the course of two weeks Mike Phillips, a scrum-half for Ospreys and Wales, and Lesley Vainikolo, a wing for Gloucester and England, were involved in incidents outside nightclubs. The Tongan born, New Zealand rugby league international Vainikolo presents an appropriate point of departure here. For if a small number of players have found wider fame through the increased professionalization and commercialization of rugby union, a much larger number have experienced greater opportunities to experience new cultures and lifestyles in the period since 1995. It is to the subject of player migration that I now turn.

5
Player Migration in the Professional Age

In November 2008 the Irish province of Munster faced the New Zealand touring team. One of the great spectacles of rugby union is when the All Blacks perform their famous haka (Jackson and Hokowhitu, 2002) but before the game started the four New Zealanders in the Munster squad carried out their own haka. Doug Howlett, Rua Tipoki, Lifeimi Mafi and Jeremy Manning performed the haka while their teammates locked arms in support behind them. Tipoki, a former New Zealand Maori captain, noted that 'As a Kiwi boy you grow up hoping that you are going to play for the All Blacks one day and as a Maori to do the haka for the All Blacks.' If that was not possible then this was the next best thing.

New Zealanders performing a haka wearing the red shirt of Munster, featuring the logo of German sportswear manufacturer Adidas, emblazoned across the front with the name of the Japanese car manufacturer Toyota, offers a visible image of globalization. This example also presents a couple of interesting points to consider when we look at the role of transnational corporations today. A report in *Fortune Magazine* (23 July 2007) that compared nations with transnational corporations highlighted that the GDP of Ireland was less than the revenue of Toyota. Munster's opponents also wore shirts bearing the logo of Adidas. The 'Adidasification' of the All Blacks represented the biggest commercial branding in world rugby and also created much controversy in New Zealand (Jackson, Batty and Scherer, 2001). The fact that the All Blacks were in Munster at all was also an interesting story. The match was billed as something to commemorate the thirtieth anniversary of Munster's defeat of New Zealand in 1978 (English, 2007). RTE Sport (28 April 2008) reported the New Zealand Rugby Football Union (NZRFU)

Chief Executive's comment that the game 'has commercial benefits for both teams' and also noted how the NZRFU are 'seeking new ways to generate revenue in an effort to stymie player drain to rich European clubs'. The fact that the New Zealand team was there at all hardly registered in most accounts although an article the *Guardian* (28 July 2009) on the location of forthcoming rugby world cups noted that

> [j]ust when it seemed rugby was about to expand beyond the circle of founding fathers and opt for Japan in 2011, the Kiwis fixed a deal to play a game in Munster and lo and behold the vote swung New Zealand's way.

Traditional tours where national teams would play against clubs and/or representative sides, in addition to their international fixtures, occur less and less in the contemporary game and for many commentators are one of the biggest losses of the open era (McRae, 2007; Nicholls, 2006). In comparing the New Zealand tours of 1905 and 2005, Lewis and Winder (2007) draw attention to the fact the 1905 tour is used as a benchmark for each new generation of All Blacks and that this tour continues to be read in colonial and nostalgic terms. Of the players who made up the 1905 touring party only two were born outside New Zealand and one of these, the revered captain Gallaher, died fighting for his adopted country. The 2005 All Blacks included ten players born outside the country (nine of whom were born in the Pacific Islands) and were captained for the first time by a player (Tana Umaga) of Pacific Island ethnicity. Tana's brother, Mike, had represented Samoa in international rugby and the two even played against each other for these nations. The relationship between New Zealand and Samoa will be looked at in more detail in Chapter 7 as it offers an interesting site for examining an aspect of labour migration in sport that has received little attention to date (Grainger, 2006). To help frame the next three chapters, and the key issues impacting upon the contemporary rugby world, the section below provides a brief synopsis of some of the important work already undertaken on labour migration in sport.

Labour migration, typologies and theories

Scholars have commented on and examined patterns of labour migration in a variety of sports over the course of the past two decades (see especially, Bale, 1991; Bale and Maguire, 1994; Klein, 2006; Lanfranchi and Taylor, 2001; Maguire, 1999). In the contemporary sporting world it is clear that the movement of athletes traverse geographical, political, cultural, ethnic and economic boundaries. These flows have developed over time with the increasing globalization of top-level sports (Klein, 2006; Lanfranchi and Taylor, 2001; Maguire, 1999). The increased migration of athletes has allowed researchers to map the patterns of movement between what are often termed host and donor countries (Maguire, 1999). The movement of athletes from a donor country to a host country varies depending upon the sport. However, movement can increasingly be seen to be taking place through a series of talent pipelines both in terms of changes for club/regional teams but also, somewhat more controversially, for increasing the quality of national teams in a variety of sports. Yet we must be careful not to make any generalizations about these migratory patterns for these movements may change markedly across sports. Therefore while many New Zealand rugby players make the move to Japan to play the game (Chiba and Jackson, 2006; Howitt and Haworth, 2002; Sakata, 2004) the same country is also host to a number of Brazilians who migrate there to play association football (Giulianotti and Robertson, 2009).

In an attempt to frame the manner in which athletes engage with the migration experience, scholars have developed typologies of sport labour migration (e.g. Magee and Sugden, 2002; Maguire, 1996). Maguire (1996) described the movement of athletes within a model built upon five overlapping categories that frame the complex interplay of multidirectional processes. He suggests that the migration experience is characterized by a mix of overlapping processes exemplified by groups he characterizes as *pioneers, mercenaries, nomadic cosmopolitans, settlers* and *returnees* (Maguire, 1996). Magee and Sugden (2002) added to Maguire's (1996) typology by introducing the categories of *ambitionist, exile* and *expelled*. Before looking at specific aspects of migration in rugby it is worth identifying and outlining the categories employed here.

The *pioneer* type migrant will engage with the migration process in an attempt to promote their sport. These migrants will use the migration experience in an attempt to encourage others to become involved and the early spread of rugby to parts of the British Empire can be seen as an early example of this. By contrast, *mercenaries*, rather than wishing to develop their sport in a foreign land, will be more highly motivated by short term, usually financially oriented, goals. They will, therefore, spend little time with a specific team or club before moving elsewhere in order to secure the most lucrative deal. Media accounts in many of the leading rugby-playing nations attest to the perceived mercenary culture encompassing the professional game. The large number of high profile southern hemisphere players moving to England towards the end of their careers were often portrayed as mercenaries and were viewed as having a negative impact on the game in the country. The *nomadic cosmopolitan* will seek a more cultural engagement with the migration experience, rather than just a financial one. The migration experience, for these workers, is based upon the ability to travel and to experience and engage with new cosmopolitan encounters. Players moving from the British Isles to France citing the change of lifestyle as a key factor in their decision, is a good example of this and is a subject I will return to in this chapter.

The *settler* is less likely to seek transient cultural encounters. Athletes in this category will use the migration experience, either intentionally, or unintentionally, to shift their permanent residence. The experiences of some Tongan rugby players in Wales illustrate this (Williams, 2004) and in a few years' time the Welsh national team may well feature players of Tongan descent in their match-day squads as the children of some of these settlers are schooled in the country. Many of these boys are seen as having a distinct advantage in schools rugby in New Zealand where it has been suggested that the size of Pacific Island players is driving others away from the game (Teaiwa and Mallon, 2005). In the winter of 2009 an under-18 trial match to decide on the Welsh squad for the forthcoming season featured the son of one of these former Tongan internationals.

The returnee will not settle in the country to which they have moved and will have completed a full-circle in respect of their migration when they return home to ply their trade. Many examples fall into the above including the Rhodesian-born and Durban-educated Andy Marinos who represented Wales in international rugby but is now a senior figure in the South Africa Rugby Football Union and part of his role will involve trying to keep South African players in the country. For the ambitionist, migration occurs because of their desire to secure a professional playing opportunity anywhere, irrespective of the locality or the quality of the league. Certain ambitionist migrants might also have desires to play in leagues commensurate with their own abilities. The international rugby community includes many, and varied, cases of players who have achieved full international honours in a country different from that in which they were born. In many cases, it could be argued that, they would never have achieved international honours in their home nation (see Chapter 7). Perhaps the fact that 27 New Zealand–born players featured in the 2007 World Cup squads for nations other than their home country demonstrates this best. The *exile* is a migrant who due to any one of a number of reasons (professional an/or personal) decides to leave one country for another. The *expelled* migrant, however, does not migrate voluntarily. For these migrants' movements from one nation to another are usually the result of some sort of behavioural and/or media exposure-related problem at some point during their career in a particular place. As identified in Chapter 3 the open professionalization of rugby union made this an option for movement between the two codes in such a scenario.

The motivations and experiences of athletic migrants vary considerably (Bale, 1991; Klein, 2006; Maguire, 1996). The migration experience is underpinned by a series of complex interdependent processes. Politics, history, economics, geography and culture are all instrumental in determining both the motivations of migrants and in affecting the ways in which they experience the migration process (Delanty, Wodak and Jones, 2008). Research has shown that a number of interdependent processes frame each specific migratory experience. While there is much valuable research into the subject it is obvious that much of the migration is clearly defined by economic factors (e.g. Grainger, 2006; Teaiwa and Mallon, 2005; Magee, 2006) although as Elliott and Maguire (2008) suggest it is important that future studies try and better understand these processes by introducing a conceptual synthesis that draws upon research from other areas of highly skilled labour migration.

It is also important to acknowledge that the movement of athletic migrants does not always occur towards the 'core' for migration occurs on a number of levels and for a variety of different reasons although it is clear that in rugby union we are largely witnessing a movement of athletes between a relatively small number of nations. In many cases globalization is used as a 'catch-all' term to describe migration when in reality, as McGovern (2002) has cogently stated, it may be more pertinent to refer instead to internationalization. His research on the migration of footballers to the English league clearly highlights that migration occurs largely across much more limited lines and tends to favour foreign sources that most resemble local sources. Of course it is important to note that since McGovern's (2002) work was published there has been an expansion in the international growth of English football. In the inaugural season of the English Premier League there were just 11 'foreign' players registered with clubs but by the start of the 2008–9 season there were over 300 'foreign' players from more than 60 different nations. The leading rugby league in England has nothing like as wide a reach and only 17 different nations were represented in the squads of clubs at the start of the 2009–10 season. This 17 includes the other home nations and generally includes players solely from the nations discussed in this text where rugby has some type of significant presence in the sporting landscape. It also incorporates a strange anomaly with the presence of a Norwegian international (a nation ranked 78 in the world) although it should be noted that Erik Lund moved to England when he was six months old and has played all of his club rugby in England where his brother Magnus has achieved international honours for the English national team.

The local in professional rugby

Rugby remained located in the local much longer than football which having been openly professional since 1885 had seen a gradual shift to become the huge commercial industry it is today (see, for example, Augustin, 1999; Howe, 1999). In recent times the figure of Rupert Murdoch looms large once again here for it was his purchase of television rights to top-level football in England that drastically altered the landscape of top-level European football. The creation of the Premier League in 1992 altered the football industry and was a key factor in the remarkable transformation of English football from what was regarded as something of a slum sport in the mid-1980s to a massive global phenomenon a decade on (Bower, 2003; J. Williams, 1994). Part of the reaction to the increased commercialization and suggested gentrification of football in the 1990s was a lamentation for the loss of a sense of identity and place. A widespread nostalgia and a visible commentary on the loss of place became quite a powerful narrative at a time when many fans felt increasingly isolated and alienated from their clubs (Bower, 2003; Giulianotti, 1999; Wagg, 2004).

Bale (2003) notes how sport exists in time and space and that teams usually represent a particular place. People identify with a place through sport, arguably more so than through any other form of culture (Bairner, 2009; Bale, 2003). Bale (1994) has also highlighted how the sports stadium is often presented as a sacred place projecting a kind of spirituality among its congregation. The term 'sacred turf' is widely used to describe the importance of sporting fields (Bale, 1994) where a love of a particular stadium is also essentially about an authentic sense of place and a sense of belonging. The fact that sports places are also treated like religious spaces helps explain their sense of topophilia – a love of place (Bale, 1994, 2003).

Topophilia was a visible theme in the media narratives surrounding the death of the former Welsh rugby union international Ray Gravell in 2007 and clearly highlighted the importance of place and local identity in rugby. A public service held at Stradey Park, the longtime home of Gravell's beloved Llanelli (Scarlets), included the scoreboard at the ground displaying the result from the famous match in 1972 when Gravell was the youngest member of the Llanelli team which defeated the All Blacks (Llanelli 9 – Zeland Newydd 3). In rugby's open era, in terms of playing squads, coaching staff and even the ownership of clubs, there is a move even further away from the local although this process is not as pronounced as is the case in English football. However, there is some evidence that in certain places this could be changing and Saracens RFC played a match against the Springboks in 2009 where they included many South Africans of their own in the team. Rugby in many of the European nations has not been affected by the Bosman ruling and the law that allows for free-dom of movement between European Union (EU) member nations for the game is played at a good standard in so few nations. Of more impact is the Kolpak ruling where a Slovakian handball player won a landmark case in the European Court of Justice for the right to play in the German handball league. Seven New Zealanders, many on European passports, were in the Northampton team in 2006. The broader trade agreement, the Contonu agreement, allows nationals of nations considered to be 'developing' the freedom to work in the EU and helps explain the large number of South African players in teams such as Saracens as identified above. Coached by a former Springbok international, under the ownership of a South African investment company, this represents another marked shift for a club and some media have taken to referring to the team as SArries to clearly outline the extent of this influence.

It would be wrong to draw a line from 1995 and suggest that it was only after open professionalization that rugby players moved from country to country. Indeed it was the relaxed approach to amateurism that tempted many players to move country throughout the history of the game. Similar to the much better paid players of today the official line was that an individual was 'moving to experience a new culture and way of life' although of course the financial rewards on offer made this a much easier choice to make. The former England centre Will Greenwood spent the first few years of his life living in Italy as his father played 'pseudo-pro, or shamateur, rugby' (Greenwood, 2005: p. 6). England's world cup–winning coach Clive Woodward had spent time as a player for the Manly club in Australia during the 1980s.

Canadian international Gareth Rees played for clubs in England, France and Wales after having attended Harrow school. Rees played in both the amateur and professional eras and appeared in all four of the first rugby world cup competitions. He also earned an Oxford Blue where of course the social status attached to competency in the gentleman's game saw to it that quality rugby players gained entry into the premier seats of learning in England even if their academic profile wasn't as strong as one would expect. In addition to the many top British and Irish players who enjoyed an Oxbridge education, teams for the annual varsity match contained representatives from Australia, New Zealand and South Africa long before the age of open professionalism. The Oxford University squad for the 2008–9 season featured players from Australia, New Zealand and South Africa, and also included a Canadian and two Americans. Of course the nations represented here reflect established patterns and the narrow lines of movement.

As referred to when discussing the passing of Ray Gravell, many rugby clubs were centered on a sense of community and built upon a strong appreciation of place (Howe, 1999; O'Brien and Slack, 2004; A. Smith, 1999). Few symbolized this local identity more than Gloucester RFC in the west of England who became an important symbol of the city. During the 1995–6 season all but one of the starting 15 of the Gloucester team were men who were local to the area. During the 2009–10 season the squad included far less local men and the English contingent were supplemented with players from Fiji, France, Italy, New Zealand, Samoa and South Africa. A Welshman has captained the team during this season and a look at the coaching staff highlights that they are currently led by a Scotsman and like many other coaching staffs around the world there is also an ex-rugby league player on the management team (see Chapter 6 for a more detailed discussion of this particular development). For a club so firmly entrenched and embedded within notions of 'the local' this represents a marked shift that took place in a short period of time. Gloucester had previously been coached by the former French international, Phillipe Saint-Andre, who had initially joined the club as a player in the early years of professionalism. Howe's (1999, 2001) research on Pontypridd RFC in Wales also showed the importance of place and the special sense of affiliation players felt with the town and the 'valley commandoes' became an important symbol of Pontypridd itself (see also, Williams, 2009). Of course this is not meant to over-simplify the differences and it is important to note that in the age before open professionalism those not from the immediate area would have played for various clubs but what cannot be disputed is that many organizations became markedly less local through the advent of professionalism (Augustin, 1999; Bateman, 2001; Catt, 2007; Daniell, 2009).

Such changes in the local composition of clubs represents interesting food for thought when considering the commonly used phrase of having 'pride in the jersey' that is so prevalent within the game. Daniell (2009) notes how in France this is referred to as *l'esprit de clocher*. A *clocher* is a church's clock tower and so symbolically the phrase stands for everything that a Frenchman should hold close to his heart – family, friends, his town – the very roots of his existence. Asserting local pride formed a fundamental aspect of identity in rugby clubs throughout the world. As a schoolboy my biggest matches were always against those of neighbouring schools. At the international level it is always victory over England that Welshmen (and women) celebrate the most. Much of our collective identities is created by identifying who we are like (and by association who we are not). The controversies relating to passports of convenience will be looked at in Chapter 7 but at the club/regional level also, as Daniell

(2009: p. 5) notes, 'you can only really have pride in the jersey if the jersey, and what it stands for, means something to you, otherwise it's just another jersey, black, white, red, blue, multicoloured or whatever'. The changes brought about by an open game can be visibly seen by looking at the case of Gloucester who within a short period of time were able to field All Black legend Ian Jones and Australia's world cup–winning centre Jason Little. Backed by the financial power of Tom Walkinshaw Gloucester, like many of the English clubs, embraced professionalism through the backing of rich benefactors. Gloucester was not the richest club though as Sir John Hall's early investment in Newcastle and Nigel Wray's spending at Saracens ensured that these two clubs claimed silverware early on in the professional era. As soon as the game became openly professional it was money that dominated most discussions and many clubs were to feel the effects of trying to buy success at all levels of the game.

Show me the money: The language of professionalism

As rugby went openly professional the financial rewards on offer with some of the English clubs were hard to turn down despite pressure from the administrators of the game for players to remain in, or in some cases return to, their home country. As indicated earlier, the former Wales Number 8 and successful Wigan RL player Scott Quinnell chose to move to England when the game went professional despite the concerted attempts to have him return to Wales. Other Welshmen joining him in the leafy suburbs of Richmond were his brother Craig, front-row forwards John Davies and Barry Williams, half-backs Adrian Davies and Andy Moore and another returnee from rugby league, Allan Bateman. Such movement created much anxiety in Wales as the WRU wanted their best players to remain in Wales and hoped that once the game went professional those who had left to join rugby league clubs would return to the Principality. Bateman (2001) notes the tensions inherent within the political wrangling of English-based players being released for international fixtures and the like.

For a period there were numerous Scottish internationals on the books of Newcastle who under the direction of Sir John Hall made the former Wigan rugby league player, and Samoa and New Zealand rugby union international, Inga Tuigimala the first million pound rugby union player (David Campese excluded!) when signing the winger to a four-year contract. Indeed it was Hall's recruitment of the then England outside-half Rob Andrew that sparked realization for many in the game that professionalism was taking place there and now. The close proximity of the club to the Scottish border meant that Newcastle also fielded a number of the top Scottish international players such as Gary Armstrong and Doddie Weir.

Through the backing of rich businessmen, large sums of money were paid to some players in England (Malin, 1997; Smith, 2000). Part of the problem with managing the financial side of the game was that professionalism happened so quickly, that many clubs panicked and offered exorbitant salaries to get players to their clubs (Edwards, 2003). O'Brien and Slack (2004) highlight the lack of strategic planning in the sport for few clubs had any real understanding of value and what appropriate market rates were. The English game, with the backing of wealthy benefactors such as Sir John Hall, Nigel Wray and Tom Walkinshaw was much richer than the sport in any of the other leading rugby nations and so was able to offer markedly more lucrative contracts than anywhere else. As dual code international Allan Bateman (2001: p. 90) noted:

> Professionalism in union seemed to revolve around pay rather than attitude. I was surprised at the high rates of pay: six-figure contracts were offered with abandon, virtually double the wages of established rugby league players. It reflected the involvement of benefactors in union, but it meant that salary levels, which were not weighted towards bonuses, were unrealistic.

Of course it is important to note here that the money was being provided by clubs and at the largesse of businessmen and not the national union. This was to be the basis of much conflict in the early years of change (Smith, 2000). It was not just the financial rewards that tempted players to England. Many were also motivated by the chance to play at a higher level and with what was perceived as a lack of any clear vision or direction in neighbouring Scotland or Wales, many top players had spells with English clubs. As the largest and wealthiest rugby market England was able to attract some of the biggest names in world rugby; so within a short period of time many of the most recognizable names in the sport could be found playing in the English league. In addition to luminaries such as Michael Lynagh, Ian Jones and Francois Pienaar from the SANZAR region players such as Augustin Pichot (Argentina), Phillipe Sella (France) and Keith Wood (Ireland) also made the move to England. Of course part of the problem in theorizing issues around migration is that while players may state that they are not moving 'just for the money' this is an easy statement to make when an athlete receives a significant financial recompense for doing so. Such proclamations of athletes are taken with a pinch of salt – as much as non-national players who claim to be fulfilling a boyhood dream when first being selected for their adopted country! Club versus country rows became a staple feature of discussions in all parts of the rugby world and continues to this day.

Border crossing: Across the Channel and from South to North

In February 2009 the English side London Wasps announced that three of its players, and current England squad members, would be leaving the club to pursue opportunities in France. The transfers of Tom Palmer and James Haskell to Stade Francais and that of Riki Flutey to Brive attracted widespread media attention. Haskell in particular seemed somewhat ostracized when having previously been touted as a potential future captain of the national team he was excluded from both the elite England squad and the England Saxons squad at the start of the 2009–10 season. England's most famous player also made the move south to sign for Toulon during this time although Jonny Wilkinson's move is largely presented in a positive fashion and early signs suggest it has been a good move for the injury-plagued player.

In addition to the obvious linguistic differences the type of rugby played in France and the culture that surrounds it is arguably more distinct than that played anywhere else (see for example, Daniell, 2009; Dine, 2001). The New Zealander Tabai Matson recalls his introduction to the Brive club in France where he witnessed the team coach stagger off the field with a bleeding nose following a confrontation with a player. As his Scottish teammate Gregor Townsend explained, 'the coach is a nutter ... he motivates his players before a match by shouting at them, abusing and punching them' (in Howitt and Haworth, 2002: p. 163). On this particular occasion the player had reacted and the two of them, much to the coach's obvious enjoyment, fought each other.

The salary cap in the English game was cited as a reason why some chose to pursue greater financial rewards across the English Channel. The somewhat relaxed approach to amateurism had attracted players for decades but many were also tempted by the very different lifestyle on offer in the south of the country in particular. In the openly professional age, with the migration of players from a wider selection of nations, we saw a more international make-up to the Top 14 in France. Players from 25 other nations were contracted to French clubs at the start of the 2009–10 season. As a reflection of the marked shift and internationalization of the domestic game in France, Welshman Alix Popham was appointed captain of Brive for the 2009–10 season to lead a squad with more overseas players than Frenchmen. Owing to the massive number of foreign players at the club some of the French players undertook English lessons so they would be able to better communicate with their teammates.

Whereas the southern hemisphere nations have led the way in the professionalization of the game and have been dominant in world cup competitions, winning five of the six world cups to date, there is little doubt that in playing terms the northern hemisphere represents an increasingly powerful economic core. Although it is not really a fair comparison, given the limited time that they have to prepare to take on their opponents, it is also worth noting that the British and Irish Lions have lost all three of the last test series against the southern hemisphere's leading teams. Yet in economic terms the power base is very much in the northern hemisphere. The southern hemisphere nations have enforced strict controls with regard to players remaining in their home country in order to be eligible to play for the national team. Yet the financial rewards on offer from some of the main French and English clubs in particular has meant that some players chose to relinquish their jersey or give up hope of progressing to the senior national team for better economic conditions abroad. In the early years of professionalism England (and other parts of Europe) represented a place for southern hemisphere players moving towards the end of their international careers to come and have one last big payday. Yet after the 2007 World Cup commentators noted the increasing number of younger internationals being tempted abroad, many of whom were near their peak as players and close to being certainties to remain part of their national 15 for many years.

The career of the professional rugby player is typically a pretty short one so opportunities to make money from the game are few and far between. Only a handful of players (e.g. Jonah Lomu and Jonny Wilkinson) could earn enough from the sport and related commercial endorsements to never have to work once their career as professional rugby players had finished. Howitt and Haworth (2002) have highlighted how players from New Zealand migrated to various parts of the world. As a nation defined by rugby, represented by a brand that promotes and portrays the nation overseas (Gilson et al., 2000; Scherer and Jackson, 2008), it is no surprise to note the prevalence of New Zealand players in a number of countries. Despite the widespread criticism of their so-called pillaging of the South Sea Islands to strengthen their national team there were more athletes born in New Zealand playing in the 2007 world cup than there were from any other country.

An article in *The Sunday Times* (29 April 2007) noted how northern market forces are now dominating the international game and referred to a player exodus that would drastically alter the landscape of the professional game:

> This exodus represents the biggest sea-change in the game since it turned professional 12 years ago, and threatens to turn the world order on its head. Until now it has been a rarity for any player from the SANZAR unions to take up a northern contract until they have called time on their international career.

The New Zealand prop Carl Hayman signed for Newcastle Falcons in England for a reputed 350,000 British pounds a season (approximately double of what he could earn at home). While this represents a massive amount for a rugby player and reputedly made Hayman the highest earner in the sport, it is worth noting that it is about two to three weeks' wages for a top premier league football player. Even before the open professionalization of the game many New Zealanders had moved to Japan where companies were willing to pay large sums of money to quality rugby players. Daniell (2009) states that when he first began to play professional rugby in France in 1997 he was part of a trickle of New Zealanders but that movement now resembles a flood and by 2009 top All Blacks players such as Tana Umaga and Byron Kelleher had signed lucrative contracts with clubs in France. Using a similar terminology *The Sunday Times* (29 April 2007) referred to these migration patterns as a trickle that was 'now becoming a torrent'. A look at the playing squads of clubs in the top-level of English and French rugby highlights that a number of players from the southern hemisphere now ply their trade in these two nations; and at the start of the 2009–10 season, there were over one hundred southern hemisphere players in France and close to this amount in England. The fear of losing their best players as more and more chose to develop their career (and bank balance) overseas meant that the NZRFU had to make some allowances. Daniel Carter, the outstanding All Blacks outside-half, was given permission to take a 'rugby sabbatical' and signed a six month contract with Perpignan in France for a reported 35,000 Euros a game although injury meant that his stay was cut short and he only featured in five games. In a newspaper interview prior to his departure he noted how he had turned down an offer from Toulon where there were already seven other New Zealanders in the playing squad and others on the coaching staff noting that 'I didn't want to immerse myself in a Kiwi environment' (*Telegraph*, 22 September 2008).

In addition to the high profile signings of Jonathan Davies and Iestyn Harris discussed in Chapter 3, Cardiff RFC, as the wealthiest club in Wales, were able to secure the services of quality overseas players such as Pieter Muller (South Africa) and Dan Baugh (Canada). The migration of players from countries such as Tonga and South Africa into the Welsh club/regional game provides visible examples of an ever-changing landscape and an insight into the increased internationalization of the sport. The number of overseas players making their living in rugby playing nations across the world continues to provoke much debate and is often cited as being a key factor in the poor performances of national teams. Prior to the creation of regional teams in 2003 the nine top-flight clubs in Wales had around 50 foreign players on their books. An article in *The Western Mail* (14 November 2007) described this as 'the dog days of the nine-club top-flight when we were swamped by a host of Canadians, Americans and south sea islanders of distinctly dubious quality'. Although it is generally agreed that the quality of the overseas imports is on the whole higher than was previously the case, with only four regional teams now making up the top tier of rugby in the Principality, much debate continues to centre upon the place of non-national players in the domestic game here and in all other nations where there is a large inward migration.

In the shadow of Cardiff lies the city of Newport. Jones (2000: p. 211) notes how Newport RFC, once a leading power in the game, had long-since ceased to be a major force:

> Amateurism not only meant not paying players, you see. It meant allowing great institutions to atrophy, to slow to a crawl against the brush of conservatism and cobwebs. For the previous twenty years, Newport had not the remotest grasp of rugby's progress, it's new marketing theories. Newport stood there, hidebound, and expected top players and companies to come to them – not because they had much to offer, just because they *were* Newport.

What they did have to offer in the professional age was money. Under the leadership of Tony Brown a massive investment of capital saw Newport sign some leading rugby players. The Fijian Simon Raiwalui moved to Newport from Sale along with New Zealander, and soon to be Wales international, Shane Howarth (see also, Chapter 7). South African international players such as Gary Teichman and Percy Montgomery also moved to Newport. The signing of Teichman, in particular, was regarded as a major coup for the area and he was instrumental in helping develop some of the younger Welsh players during his time in the country. Teichman had captained South Africa and was described as 'one of the most important figures in world rugby' (Jones, 2000: p. 211).

Magee's (2006) research based upon interviews with nine South African players who had moved to the Principality highlights the various 'push' and 'pull' factors that had brought these players to Wales. Magee identifies three main ways by which players were recruited to come and play for Welsh clubs. Firstly, there were those who were approached through players and/or coaches they knew from their homeland who were already in Wales. Some were contacted through an agency that had been set up for South African sportsmen. Others were identified on the basis of ancestral links to Wales and so were recruited with the aim of one day representing the national team. Financial incentives were of course a key factor in bringing South African players to Wales. Safety issues in their home country and concerns over the quota system being introduced into their domestic game were also major motivating factors for some of the players to move overseas (Magee, 2006). In his autobiography South Africa's 2007 world cup–winning coach Jake White (2007) outlines some of the challenges he faced in negotiating this issue and the pressure exerted by a number of those involved in the governance of the game.

Tongan players' motivations for migrating to Wales had some similarities with their South African counterparts in that financial rewards were identified as important (Williams, 2004). Yet what many Tongans identified as one of the key reasons for their moving to Wales was the quality of the school system and the importance attached to providing their children with a good education. Some also talked of their aspirations for life after their rugby careers had finished and the way in which a better life could be had in Wales. As one player noted with regard to his opportunities back in Tonga when his playing career was over 'after rugby what do you do? You do nothing, well you either go fishing or back to the bush' (Williams, 2004). The impact of professionalism on some of the poorer rugby-playing nations is a subject I will consider in more depth in Chapter 7 but represents an appropriate point of departure here to consider some of the wider issues relating to migration.

Core and periphery: Power, change and the international game

Many players from some of the poorer rugby nations found themselves unable to compete in the 2003 world cup finals. Unlike in many other major sports the domestic competitions continue in some nations when the world cup is being played. Some of the most successful clubs, who provide a large number of internationals to national teams lose the services of their best players for a significant part of the season. Yet of most concern is the fact that some of the poorer rugby nations are unable to make up the wages players would lose by representing their country. An article in the *New York Times* (7 October 2003) described this as 'the Third World players stay behind at the clubs, doing the work of the First World players who are at the World Cup'. In this sense then it is apparent that rugby's globalization, or more accurately its internationalization, has been considerably affected by professionalism in a most negative way. While there may well be a greater movement of athletes between the rugby-playing nations the increasing gap caused by those with money and those without means that players might have had to put their monetary concerns ahead of international commitments. This gap has now become an obvious gulf so in addition to some of the issues discussed in Chapter 7 relating to the changing national affiliations of players, it is clear that clubs in the richest nations can sometimes prevent players from the poorest nations from representing their country. Research has shown that on average clubs in England will have 18 percent of players unavailable for any particular match due to injuries (Brooks et al., 2005). Such research powerfully highlights how clubs sometimes exert pressure on players to not turn out for their countries. This also points to the high rates of injury in the professional game and the knowledge for all players that they may be one game away from a career-ending injury.

As a nation outside the core, Argentina represents a particularly interesting case to consider. Neither part of the Tri-Nations or Six Nations tournaments, they became the first nation outside the core to reach the semi-finals of a world cup in 2007. Much debate surrounded discussions of how to incorporate the Pumas with some suggesting that they should be added to the Six Nations competition while others put forward the case for the country to join the southern hemisphere rugby giants. The Argentina squad that competed in the 2007 world cup finals included just seven players who played their club rugby in the country. This was just a couple more than played in England and less than half the number of Argentinean internationals playing for French clubs at this time. With one player in Ireland and one in Italy more than three-quarters of the squad were contracted to European clubs. At the start of the 2009–10 season 33 Argentinean players were contracted to clubs in the Guinness Premiership (England) and Top 14 competition in France. In 2009 it was announced that Argentina would be invited to join an expanded tournament with the Tri-Nations but this was subject to certain conditions being met. One of these concerned securing the requisite approval of media corporations who of course were integral in the inception of the tournament but the other condition was that the ARU could guarantee that their best players would be able to play in the expanded Super 15 competition.

Argentina's proposed inclusion was described as the Tri-Nations receiving 'a much-needed jolt' (*The Sydney Morning Herald*, 14 September 2009). Several discourses are directing their attention to the global geography of the invitation wanting to see a truly southern hemisphere championship and perhaps challenge the far more established Six Nations tournament in the international game or the increasingly popular Heineken Cup in the club/regional game. An article in *The Australian* (15 September 2009) points out that Argentina's previous international performances beyond their World Cup success, highlight that the Pumas have been more successful against Six-Nations teams as opposed to the Tri-Nations teams. This makes sense when one considers where the majority of Argentina's top players have been playing their rugby. Argentina could be viewed as providing a contrast in playing style to the three existing teams, with the goal of attracting more attention and a broader audience of supporters, both internationally and within Argentina. It is not yet clear if, and how, the leading Argentinean players will be incorporated into the Super 15 tournament but the development represents an exciting and progressive change in the sport and a significant step towards expanding the game.

In total 140 players on duty at the 2007 world cup were signed to French clubs and there were as many Georgian internationals as there were Frenchmen earning a living playing rugby in France in these squads. As many as 18 Romanian internationals also played in France. The country with the second highest number of players at the tournament was England with four times as many Samoan squad members and three times as many Fijians playing in the country than there were in New Zealand. This figure does not of course take into account the players of Fijian and Samoan birth representing New Zealand and I will consider this subject more closely in Chapter 7. There were 13 Namibian players working as professional rugby players in South Africa; and in total of the 20 nations taking part only four comprised solely of players registered to clubs in that country (Australia, New Zealand, Japan and South Africa). As indicated previously the three giants of the southern hemisphere all enforce policies that only select players based in the country for the national teams. Interestingly, as will be discussed in Chapter 7, despite the fact that these four nations comprised solely of players contracted to clubs in their respective countries none of these nations consisted solely of players born in the country.

The complexity of migrant motivation can also be linked to a lack of opportunity for career development in an athlete's home nation. The lack of professional opportunity may push the athlete from their home nation, while the lure of a specific location may pull them in a particular direction (on cultural or economic grounds). As indicated earlier, the published research on labour migration typologies have been developed to help explain the migration patterns of athletes (Maguire, 1996; Magee and Sugden, 2002). These typologies have been the subject of some contention and debate between groups of scholars yet, as Maguire (2004: p. 480) has more recently suggested, typologies 'are ideal representations of the real world and that it would be foolish to see their categories as either mutually exclusive or set in stone'. Informal networks are prevalent in the recruitment process and not all moves are planned or intentional but emerge in varied ways. The South African–born Mike Catt moved to England, where his mother was from, initially on a visit but ended up staying and winning the world cup as an England player. John Leslie, the New Zealand–born Scottish international, first went to play rugby in Japan on the recommendation of his good friend Jamie Joseph who was already well established at the Sanix Club. Chiba and Jackson's (2006) work provides some interesting insights on this movement between New Zealand and Japan although the published academic research and (auto)biographies of top players evidence that each individual has a different tale to tell and many players would fall into any number of the categories identified in academic research on labour migration typologies.

As it stands the dynamics of the rugby world continue to evolve rapidly. Concern in England over the movement of national squad members to France pales in comparison to the increased movement of southern hemisphere players to the northern hemisphere where, if current trends continue (and certainly in light of the recent economic downturn many expect it to), this may seriously devalue the profile and status of the Tri-Nations and Super 14 tournaments. These concerns were evidenced by the decision to grant Daniel Carter a 'sabbatical' so that he could capitalize on his earning potential yet still remain a part of the New Zealand squad aiming to win the world cup on home soil in 2011. The invitation to Argentina to join an expanded tournament and place their players with (what will then be the) Super 15 teams represents a most interesting development. Yet while the movement of athletes continues to attract much debate and forms a staple part of academic research into labour migration in a range of sports, far less attention is afforded to the movement of coaches. At the 2003 world cup six different nations had a New Zealander in the position of Head Coach. In the next chapter I look at the migration of coaches in professional rugby union and consider how this has impacted upon the sport.

6
The Migration of Coaches in Rugby Union

The geographical centre of North America is Rugby, North Dakota. In sporting terms though, in the US, rugby is very much on the periphery of a landscape dominated by what Markovits and Hellerman (2001) refer to as the big three (and a half) sports of baseball, basketball, [American] football (and [ice] hockey). If, as these authors attest, soccer is a potent symbol of American exceptionalism then rugby may also be viewed as a key symbol of difference although it is not so much the position of rugby that is important here but the hegemonic status of another code of football. Indeed the immensely popular sport of (American) football derives from rugby. Rugby in the US remains something of a minority activity and reflects the fact that America's sports exceptionalism 'is deeply rooted in other exceptionalisms that constitute essential features of modern American life' (Markovits and Hellerman, 2001: p. 9).

In 2008 USA Rugby announced the appointment of Scott Johnson as Head Coach of the national team. Johnson is often described as a 'fairdinkum Aussie', a coaching maverick who proved immensely popular with the players during his time working with the Welsh national squad (Henson, 2005; Thomas, 2007; Williams, 2009). Having represented Australia A as a player Johnson was recognized as an innovative coach who empowered players and created a stimulating training environment. The acquisition of Johnson was seen as a major coup for rugby in the US. As his appointment to the USA Eagles was confirmed Johnson commented that

> I've always been a huge advocate in the theory that the success of rugby worldwide is contingent on a strong American foothold,

and I feel privileged to get this opportunity to be a part of the development of the game on a larger scale.

Despite referring to rugby in the US as 'the last frontier' and claiming to be in the job 'for the long haul' (Planet Rugby, 2008) Johnson left the organization the following year to take up a post with the Ospreys region in Wales. Of course Johnson was lured to the US by a very attractive salary in a nation where many of the international team are in full-time employment outside of the sport. Michael Petri, the US captain, works for a wealth-management firm and like many players needs to secure long periods of time away from work. An article in *USA Today* (30 June 2009) outlined the composition of the team:

> The U.S. team is composed of amateur players who receive small per diems from USA Rugby while competing at the highest level in one of the world's most popular and dangerous sports. Ranging in age from 19 to 35, the 33-man team is a microcosm of America, counting among its players an Air Force lieutenant, college students, teachers, bankers, security guards and fathers.

On leaving his post with the USA Eagles Johnson was replaced by the Irishman Eddie O'Sullivan. O'Sullivan had once coached the Irish national team and had worked in the US some years before. Heading up the governance of USA Rugby is Nigel Melville, a former England scrum-half who had previously worked in senior positions at London Wasps and Gloucester. Prior to this many other English coaches had been involved in rugby in the country where 'there was no merit assessment in America of English rugby coaches. Just to be English in American rugby was enough' (*The Sunday Times*, 23 November 2008). Melville has stated his aim of persuading some of the many college football players who do not make it to the National Football League (NFL) after graduating from university to try and play rugby. The talent pool here would be extensive in terms of pure athletic ability although of course rugby is a very complex game that takes some time to learn. Many of the players I worked with at Kent State University had backgrounds as high school football players and a number turned to rugby because they were not big enough to progress in football at the collegiate level. Many had only been introduced to the game whilst at university and some learned the rules of the sport through playing video games!

Earlier on I noted the association between globalization and Americanization that effectively collapses the two terms to mean the same thing. Friedman (2000: p. 382) noted that 'globalization often wears Mickey Mouse ears, eats Big Macs, drinks Coke or Pepsi and does its computing on an IBM PC, using Windows 98, with a Intel Pentium II processor and a network link from Cisco systems'. Yet despite its centrality in discussions of globalization per se, in soccer and rugby terms the US is very much a peripheral nation, albeit one that those concerned with developing the economic potential of both sports want to see much closer to the core. The power of the US is a key factor in the trend towards cultural convergence – one of the key aspects of globalization. Yet as Markovits and Hellerman (2001) note, the differences between the USA and the rest of the world in the areas of sport and culture 'remain more persistent and noticeable than the similarities' (p. 3). Yet in other ways we may well discern some influence from the process of Americanization in the development of the game as a commercial product through the increased 'razzmatazz' that surrounds the sport (after Allison, 2005). A recent example to highlight this is Stade Francais who included dancing girls and medieval jousters to make matches a 'spectacle'. Here 78,000 spectators have been attracted to some games in the past couple of seasons. That represents a massive figure for a club rugby match anywhere in the world. Cheerleaders also form a part of Super 14 events where the old Super 12 was described as being about 'entertainment, flamboyance, colour and razzmatazz' (Gilson et al., 2000: p. 99) and positioned as something quite different from international fixtures.

In relation to rugby coaching the earliest rugby sides did not have coaches and the captain of the team was responsible for the nominal leadership. Later in the amateur era as coaching became more recognized the post may have been little more than a token one. In the professional era we have witnessed an increase in the number of coaches where now the top rugby teams across the world employ a raft of specialist coaches among whose number may include coaches with special responsibility for attack, defence, scrums, kicking and skills. This increasingly resembles the coaching staff of an American football team where specialized coaches focus on a specific aspect of the game. Yet while coaching may now be a credible career choice, and a potentially lucrative profession for an individual, the path to it being an accepted and valued part of the rugby world has been a long one.

The professionalization of coaching

Coaching is now a well-established profession in the sports world and the top coaches in a number of sports can now command massive salaries. In the US leading basketball and (American) football coaches at universities are often the highest paid employees of the institution attracting annual salaries of millions of dollars. In association football at the European clubs some coaches also earn seven figure sums annually, and increasingly the top coaches are highly coveted and change nations many times during the course of their careers (Wagg, 2007). In the days of amateurism coaching was a dirty word in rugby union (Wyatt, 1996) that reeked of professionalism in the eyes of many. A number of the top coaches during the amateur era came from teaching backgrounds. Carwyn James and Ian McGeechan, the successful British and Irish Lions coaches (see Chapter 8), were both teachers. Another Lions coach and former teacher Jim Telfer (2005: p. 113) noted how his experiences in the classroom influenced his work as a coach:

> One of my eccentricities, even at that time, was to make notes for all of the coaching session I conducted. ... The concept of note-making came from my experience of having to prepare lessons in school, where it was vital to ensure you had enough material to fill the full lesson.

In addition to the obvious links between teaching and coaching, which remains an area in need of further investigation, the fact that many rugby coaches in Britain were schooled in the Colleges of Education (such as Cardiff, Carnegie and Loughborough) provided a clear link to rugby coaching in its earliest days. The challenges initially faced by the open professionalization of rugby is evidenced by Clive Woodward's recollections of his time as England Head Coach. In the opening chapter of his book *Winning*, Woodward recalls his first day in the post as England's first ever full-time rugby coach.

Having arrived at Twickenham, the headquarters of the game in England, Woodward (2004: p. 2) recalls a conversation he had with the Director of the RFU:

> I'm here to start work. Normally I'll be in by 7 am, but it's only day one, so I thought I'd give you all a bit of time. I'd like to settle into my office, you know, and get things started.

Despite considering himself to be a sharp negotiator in his business life where he had built up a very successful leasing company, Woodward had neglected to negotiate for an office, phone and secretary when offered the post. The RFU had not even considered that Woodward would require an office as they had never employed a full-time coach before. This one encounter is a visible example of how the game struggled at times to cope with the change. In developing a fully 'professional' set-up for what became known as England Rugby, Woodward was often praised for being such an innovator (see for example, Catt, 2007; Dallaglio, 2007; Greenwood, 2005; Leonard, 2004). In addition to overseeing a massive overhaul of all aspects of the international environment for England's players he surrounded himself with specialist coaches charged with developing specific aspects of the game. Woodward regularly reviewed the progress of England Rugby and critically assessed just where the team was placed in terms of reaching their long-term goals. In bringing in a range of specialists from very different environments he attempted to learn more about how small parts of the overall performance could be noticeably improved by applying new ideas. Looking at the bigger picture helped Woodward contextualize just how and what needed to be developed (Woodward, 2004). This coaching team included a New Zealander and others who had previously worked in rugby league. These present an appropriate point of departure in identifying the main focus of this chapter were I look at the migration of coaches from New Zealand and then at the increased significance of former rugby league coaches in the professional union game as two key factors in the changes shaping international rugby. This is then positioned within and around the notion of sameness and difference in the international game and contemporary concerns as relates to the current positioning of the sport.

The Great Redeemer and other Kiwis abroad

> You will find New Zealand coaches in all parts of the world and at all standards. Ellis Meachen and Steve McDowell are cracking the whip in Romania, where the national team suffered from the break-up of the old Communist Bloc and is trying to revive, and there is even a Kiwi influence in the fledgling Columbian Union with the effervescent Bill Paul in charge.
>
> *(The Sunday Times,* 23 November 2008)

This quote from an English newspaper under the title 'New Zealand Coaches Leading the World' highlighted the significant presence of coaches from this one rugby nation who were making an impact on the sport in a number of countries. Some years ago Howitt and Haworth (2002) had written a book about the experiences of New Zealanders playing and coaching rugby in a range of nations across the world. The close link between rugby and images of this nation, as outlined previously, afforded the country a hegemonic status in the game. Their victory in the first ever world cup and the almost mythical status afforded to the All Blacks brand further developed this.

Following poor results after the onset of professionalism, and now not even having the (at times quite valid) excuse that the best players had all gone north to rugby league, it was clear that the Welsh national team needed a new sense of direction. In 1998 the Welsh Rugby Union secured the services of a former schoolteacher from New Zealand and Graham Henry assumed the role of Head Coach for a salary reputed to be five times that of the previous incumbent of the post. It was often suggested that Henry enjoyed the success that he did and the support of various groups within the Principality largely because he was not Welsh. Henry led the team on a long unbeaten run and was soon proclaimed as 'The Great Redeemer' reflecting both the desire for success within the Principality and the quasi-religious status of the national game. Henry was not the only overseas coach involved with the Welsh team. He brought in fellow New Zealander Steve Hansen to his coaching staff and later on Scott Johnson also joined the national set-up. Andrew Hore, also from New Zealand, was employed as Fitness Coach and after a brief spell back in his home country was to return to Wales to take up the position of Elite Performance Director of the Ospreys region.

In the winter of 2007 the WRU appointed Warren Gatland as Head Coach and he became the third New Zealander to lead the Welsh national team in less than a decade. To further highlight migration patterns in the sport Gatland had previously coached the Irish national team and English club-side London Wasps. Assisted by Englishman, and former Great Britain Rugby League international Shaun Edwards, Gatland led the team to the Grand Slam in his first season in charge. Despite this success Gatland has also voiced his concern abut the number of foreign players playing in the country and within one hour of being officially unveiled as the new coach of Wales he expressed his disquiet over the number of overseas imports and how they were preventing home-grown players from playing top-level rugby (see also Chapter 5). Of course there is some irony in a New Zealander expressing such a view in Wales.

Unlike most other nations Australia resisted looking overseas to find a new coach but one of the last frontiers was crossed when New Zealander Robbie Deans was appointed to the post of Head Coach of the Wallabies. Horton (2009: p. 979) noted that the appointment of Deans 'could be viewed as an indication that rugby union in Australia has possibly become less xenophobic and more, albeit thinly, cosmopolitan'. However, before his appointment when Deans was first linked to the post there was much negative commentary and a number of parochial comments surrounding his suitability for the job. Of course the rivalry between New Zealand and Australia made this a particularly contentious appointment for some.

John Kirwan, a star of the first word cup, where he scored one of the most memorable tries of the competition in New Zealand's defeat of Italy, has led both Italy and Japan in international rugby. Kirwan has an Italian wife who he met while spending his winters playing for the Benetton club in the (sh)amateur era. While coaching the Italian side he noted the importance of adapting to different cultural contexts and noted that 'as a foreigner, I must give them the things that I believe are good from our culture but not disturb theirs in the process' (in Howitt and Haworth, 2002: p. 188). This clearly highlights the importance of facilitating the intersection between a host culture and the knowledge base of a migrant worker that capably demonstrates the local/global interconnectedness.

Alex 'Grizz' Wylie is a renowned and respected figure in rugby circles having featured firstly as a player and then later as a successful coach of the All Blacks. He gained further international experience as coach of Argentina. As there was a strong resistance to professionalism in Argentinean rugby, Wylie initially carried the title of Technical Advisor rather than Coach and led the team in the 1999 world cup finals. As identified in the previous chapter Argentina is at a crucial stage in its development and it is important that they are given the requisite support to develop. Brad Johnstone also coached more than one nation in the international arena having held posts with both the Fijian and Italian national teams. Adapting to different cultural contexts is a key challenge in the lives of migrant players and coaches. Johnstone recalled having to broker a marriage settlement prior to one overseas tour when the wife of a Fijian player refused to release his passport (Howitt and Haworth, 2002). Johnstone's work in Fiji was constrained by the very limited funds available to develop the game thereby clearly illustrating the problems that many nations in the rugby world have faced. At the time he was employed on the island, Fiji received a $25,000 grant from the IRB and $50,000 from Vodafone as a sponsor to support all rugby there. The challenges for Fijian rugby in ensuring that the best players from the country can play for the national team will be considered further in Chapter 7.

Many other New Zealanders have also enjoyed considerable success as coaches across the world outside of the more established rugby nations. George Simpkin, for example, has worked with the national teams of Hong Kong, Fiji and Sri Lanka. During his time in Hong Kong Simpkin also did much to promote the sport in China. China remains an area that the international rugby community are keen to expand their sport into, for its population size and rising economic power makes it a target for many sports organizations. The success of basketball player Yao Ming at the Houston Rockets and the expansion of the NBA brand in China points to many of the commercial possibilities that this brings.

Numerous other New Zealanders have travelled to the corners of the rugby world and work at all levels of the game. In the days before open professionalism this was already happening (Howitt and Haworth, 2002) but now in the professional age there are an ever-increasing number of New Zealand coaches abroad. Kieran Crowley is Head Coach of Canada and John Mitchell is currently coach to the Australian side Western Force in the Super 14. I noted Mitchell's work with England early on in this chapter as they became one of the first nations to develop an extensive coaching and support squad. In addition to recognizing the benefits of bringing in people from different nations to improve players there was also a massive push to bring in some of the best coaching expertise from rugby league and this has become a defining feature of the development of most of rugby union's core nations.

In a league of their own: Defence, innovation and coach development

Numerous coaches from rugby league moved to the union game. In particular men such as Phil Larder, Clive Griffiths and Mike Ford made a significant contribution to defensive structures of international teams. The Englishman Dave Ellis worked with the French national team for a number of years as a defence coach and it was in this area of the game that former league men have had the biggest impact. Of course before the open professionalization of rugby union these league coaches would not have been permitted to work in the union game. Those individuals who made the switch from league to union as coaches were, like the men who changed codes as players, lauded for the 'professional' approach they brought to the union game. Joe Lydon noted how league coaches had looked at other sports for many years and adopted good practices by watching, studying and talking to people from these different environments (in Edwards, 2003). Rugby union, meanwhile, had been very insular and rarely looked outside of their narrow core.

Many of those who have made the transition to the union game were some of the most recogniszable names in their sport from their exploits as players in the thirteen-man game. Wigan RL greats Joe Lydon and Shaun Edwards are two former league players currently employed in senior positions within rugby union. What has yet to be considered, or analysed in any clear way, is what this tells us about the development of coaches and coaching in rugby union. The number of former rugby league men now employed in rugby union teams across the world certainly reflects the problems rugby league now faces as the union game has become the dominant commercial code (see also, Chapter 3). It also points to the limitations of coach development in the union game for large sums of money are spent on coaching and coach education yet a critical assessment would clearly indicate that key positions in many nations are often held by overseas coaches and ex-rugby league men. There is also evidence to suggest that the game is following a path prevalent in football whereby high profile players in the game are fast tracked into coaching positions with little or no understanding of coaching. Indeed as Kelly (2008) notes in research on association football an individuals status as a player is often the only criteria employed by many clubs when appointing coaches/managers. Certainly if Neil Jenkins, the first person to score more than one thousand points in international rugby and a player widely regarded as the greatest kicker in the history of the game, offers advice on kicking then you should listen. Yet, as in football, many great players are unsuited to the demands of coaching or management and fail miserably to transfer their successes as players into their role as coaches.

Conversely, as the former Welsh international Mark Ring notes, putting too much of a focus on the theoretical side at the expense of playing experience is also problematic and Ring (2006: p. 231) suggests that 'nowadays, you've got more chance of coaching a set of forwards if you've had your head stuck in a book rather than a scrum' (p. 231). Nash and Collins (2006: p. 472) state that 'coach education has to move away from the traditional classroom approach, embracing more interactive methods'. Research has shown the importance of problem solving and decision-making, neither of which can be taught or learned in a traditional way. The autobiographies of coaches such as Telfer (2005) and Woodward (2004) add further weight to this argument and highlights how very different skills are used and adapted to coach high performance teams. The stories of elite coaches highlight that individual and experiential factors are what most shaped coaching styles and philosophies. There is a definite focus on the 'art' of coaching as opposed to any established 'science' (Woodman, 1993). Research on the art of coaching is still in its infancy and there is much more to learn about the art and science of coaching elite sporting teams, particularly where this involves migrant workers.

The development of coaching reflects the many problems that continue to face the game more than a decade after the onset of open professionalism. Although people are employed to further various coach education and development initiatives there are, on the basis of appointments made at the highest levels, no clear structures or progression pathways in place in many of the leading rugby nations. Although these initiatives may appear in some official documentation, the hiring and firing of coaches, and in particular the continued trend of employing overseas coaching staff, more accurately reflect the situation.

Some of the younger Welsh coaches had taken the road out of the country to finish their playing careers and/or start coaching careers in the professional game. Former internationals Paul Turner, Phil Davies and Mark Ring all moved to England to embark on the coaching pathway. Ring (2006), in particular, has been critical of the WRU and has highlighted how the high-level coaching courses seem to focus on the 'parroting' of information and conforming to a particular model. According to Ring (2006: p. 226) 'coaches tend to get ahead because of their ability to fit into the template that is drawn up by the Welsh Rugby Union'. Numerous coaches have also left New Zealand because of their frustration with the politics governing coaching appointments in the country (Howitt and Haworth, 2002).

Those who develop successful rugby teams are likely to be innovators (see especially, Woodward, 2004). This is an interesting area in need of further research for many coach education programs seem intent on producing cardboard cutouts (Nash and Collins, 2006) and innovative ideas may be frowned upon. Innovative approaches to build winning teams featured prominently in the texts of successful coaches (e.g. Black, 2004; Telfer, 2005; White, 2007; Woodward, 2004). Clive Woodward (2004) recalled some of his earliest challenges in coaching and how he had done things 'completely my way':

> When faced with an obstacle I generally managed to sidestep it by thinking on my feet rather than confronting it head on. My approach frustrated some people, but in that regard I never really tried to work within a traditional coaching framework.
>
> (p. 12)

While many former players have been very critical of the governance and short-sightedness of unions in their own nations an added layer of complexity is added when the person is from a different country. Two main issues seem to be prevalent here. Firstly when a coach from an established rugby nation travels outside of the core the very fact that he is from the core affords an instant credibility in the host culture (Howitt and Haworth, 2002). Secondly, in some cultures that are part of the core, there is often a suspicion of difference and when a 'foreigner' comes in and tries to change the environment there can be a hostile reaction. National identities still retain an important place in sport and, as many coaches will attest, it can be a great challenge to incorporate the best of the host nation with ideas and innovations from outside these borders. Many of these ideas are of course part of a dominant direction within the game and at times this results in tensions between local styles and global trends.

There will continue to be a significant migration of coaches as rugby attempts to develop a greater international presence. Rugby is a complex sport that takes time to learn so it is no surprise to see many individuals from the core rugby nations working across the globe in a variety of roles. In the past coaches from the leading rugby nations may have occasionally travelled to undertake a coaching clinic in a 'developing' nation. Of course as alluded to previously these were not as regular an occurrence as they should have been for rugby to embrace a truly international outlook. The IRB, similar to its compatriots in FIFA or the IOC, claim to have the interests of the whole sporting community (or family in FIFA's words) at heart yet for the most part the (limited) actions speak louder than words. The history of rugby union is replete with examples whereby smaller nations are left to fend for themselves and as the game becomes more significant as an economic activity the gap between the richer and poorer rugby nations becomes more of a gulf. The cases outlined in the previous chapter concerning world cup competitions is a particularly pertinent example here to highlight the ways in which a small power elite have controlled the game.

Increasing varieties and diminishing contrasts in rugby coaching

It is interesting then to consider whether the increased migration of coaches has led to there being greater similarities in the way that teams now play. Prior to the Six Nations championship in 2008 the *Guardian* (31 January 2008) posed the question as to whether foreign coaches have 'ironed out differences between countries'. In work on globalization and sport Joseph Maguire has been one of the leading theorists to engage with issues central to the migration process (Maguire,

1994, 1996, 1999). I have already referred to this research at various points in the text although in relation to the present discussion the notion of increasing varieties and diminishing contrasts is particularly useful. Based on the work of Norbert Elias, Maguire (1994, 1996) has employed the language of increasing varieties and diminishing contrasts to illustrate the excesses of homogenization and heterogenization. Here the power dynamics between what Elias referred to as the established and the outsiders is omnipresent. Such a dynamic is clearly visible when this is applied to the contemporary rugby world where the dominance of an established core envelops the game. Yet in sport different nations are still associated with particular styles and some strive to retain these distinctive differences as global forces increasingly challenge them.

In addition to the many cases of non-nationals leading various nations (outlined above) there has also been a marked increase in the number of coaches plying their trade at club/regional level. In 2008 seven of the Guinness Premiership teams in England were led by coaches who were not English. The Australian press asked 'Where are all the Good Coaches?' in an article lamenting the fact that many leading Australian coaches were working outside of the country. This also stated that 'unless we can find a way to develop and retain Australian coaching talent, and bring some back from overseas, Australian rugby will suffer tremendously in coming years' (*Sydney Morning Herald*, 21 April 2009). An article in the *Irish Independent* (30 September 2007) reflected on the problems in identifying and developing Irish coaching talent noting the success of foreign coaches at some of the major Irish provinces. Such was the push to recruit overseas coaches during the early years of professionalism that one Dublin club employed a New Zealander whose name they didn't know and the article went on to state that 'it is only now that Irish rugby is recovering from the dizzying rush to employ foreign coaches during the 1990s'. For a period employing an Antipodean seemed to be the only way forward in many parts of British sport but not all imports were successful and Gareth Thomas (2007: p. 32) noted how his experiences with a New Zealand coach at Bridgend 'proves wrong the notion that a southern-hemisphere accent automatically makes you a rugby genius'.

Looking at the elite level of the international rugby community it is clear that there is a particularly narrow group of established coaches who have been involved with more than one of the top nations. In 1999 Graham Henry opposed his compatriot Warren Gatland when leading Wales and Ireland respectively but if that match-up was to take place now Gatland would lead Wales with Henry back home in their native New Zealand as All Blacks coach. In 2009 Gatland would have been due to face his old nemesis Eddie O'Sullivan who succeeded Gatland as Ireland coach but had now moved back to the US. Yet Gatland was in South Africa as part of the coaching squad of the British and Irish Lions. Henry had also worked with the Lions in Australia during 2001 but by the time of the next Lions tour he was in the opposition camp (see also, Chapter 8). What the above cases point to is evidence of a 'shrinking' of the rugby world and illustrates the greater interconnectedness between nations. Men such as Nick Mallet, John Kirwan, Brad Johnstone and Andy Robinson have all been Head Coach to more than one of the top 20 international sides. Others like John Mitchell, Steve Hansen and Eddie Jones have been involved in the coaching teams of more than one of the top ten nations. When this is considered alongside the increase in cross-border competition through tournaments such as the Heineken Cup and Super 14 and the increased trips that leading nations make to face each other then it is clear that there is a far greater degree of familiarity in the international game than ever before.

The expertise brought in from rugby league has added to this and contributed to the development and implementation of more sophisticated defensive structures which together with the increased training and conditioning afforded by professionalism has meant that there is less space on the field than ever before. Attacking skills have not kept pace with these developments and at present there is a real danger that many people will turn away from the game as tactical stalemates devoid of entertainment increasingly dominate.

Yet while a small number of the core rugby nations may have supplied coaches to various parts of the world there is little opportunity for coaches from the peripheral nations to further develop their skills in a core nation. In this sense then the migration of coaches into the core operates on a much narrower line than the migration of players. While the movement from core to periphery is noticeably easier for coaches it must not be forgotten that a number of athletes also move nations to play at a level more commensurate with their ability as players and so in the 2007 world cup New Zealand–born men featured in the playing squads of many nations.

In critically assessing local/global relations here there is certainly much work to be done in looking at the similarities and differences in the stories of coaches who have and haven't been successful outside their home nation. Alan Gaffney, an Australian who coached Munster, observed that while coaching South Africa Nick Mallet based their game on a strong forward pack, but when he worked with Stade Francais he went for a more expansive approach. In both cases Gaffney argues that Mallet respected what he had inherited. In Wales the criticism directed at Graham Henry during the latter part of his tenure was that he was trying to make the game too structured and his infamous pod system was too far removed from 'the Welsh way' of playing the game. More recently his fellow countryman John Kirwan has publically stated his intention for Japan to be able to compete for the trophy when they host the world cup in 2019 and that he was trying to create a Japanese style of rugby to 'change the game to suit us, not play like anyone else' (*New Zealand Herald*, 2 November 2009). As Light's (1999, 2000) research, based on his own experiences while coaching the game in Japan, has highlighted rugby in Japan is socially and culturally very different to the sport in the core nations (see also, I. Williams, 1991). Before Kirwan's appointment a number of New Zealanders had moved to Japan and ended up representing the national team. It will be interesting to observe just who is representing the nation and playing the Japanese way in 2019.

As McGovern (2002) notes, with reference to football, there is evidence that coaches/managers engage in a process that is referred to as 'homosocial reproduction' (after Kanter, 1977). Here it is suggested that in situations where performance cannot be prescribed with any confidence, managers are inclined to recruit people who are socially similar to them. It is no surprise then that with the increased migration of rugby coaches we would also see a rise in the number of players moving nations to play the game. Of course in many sports coaches who move to a different team are likely to take their trusted lieutenants with them (Wagg, 2007). This is a well-developed pattern in a range of sports and these informal networks are a key aspect of athlete and coach migration. Yet one area that has not been looked at in relation to labour migration is the conscious recruitment of players to represent a national team and it is to this issue that I now turn.

7
Passports of Convenience

My fellow countryman Ian Rush described his time playing football for Juventus as like living in a foreign country. Although he was widely mocked for making this observation, I can attest that Rushie was right as I had myself made the journey to live in Italy as a teenager. The history of sport is replete with cases of successful athletes who move away from home yet struggle to adjust to their life in a new country. Bale's (1991) work on the migration of athletes to universities in the US is a particularly good example to illustrate this. While professional athletes like Rush, and an ever increasing number of rugby players, had moved to test their skills, and experience greater financial recompense, many others have moved nations to increase their chances of attaining international honours in the game and of performing for a national team other than the country in which they were born.

To use Italy as an example, and as noted earlier, in the 2007 rugby world cup half of the Italian squad were born outside the country. Although this represented the highest number of overseas players in any one squad, most other countries' playing squads also comprised a number of players born outside national borders. New Zealand were the main exporters with 27 players born in the country representing teams other than the All Blacks. Diego Dominguez is the all-time record points scorer for the Italian national team. He was born in Argentina and toured with the national team but saw his opportunities limited because Hugo Porta, the most famous Argentinean rugby player of all time, was the incumbent of the number ten shirt. Dominguez qualified for Italy on the basis of having an Italian grandmother and became a very important player for the Azzuri. The current Italian squad includes a number of players born in Australia and New Zealand who have qualified through having a grandparent born in Italy. Italy was last led by an Italian born coach in 2000 and in the period since then has been led by a Frenchman, two New Zealanders and is currently coached by a South African. These New Zealanders, as highlighted in the previous chapter, have also coached other nations in international rugby.

At the international level the conscious recruitment of non-nationals to represent teams has also continued apace with teams comprising athletes who were born and raised thousands of miles away. Adhering to a certain playing style and aesthetic may increasingly be more problematic with so many non-national players and coaches involved in international set-ups across the globe. As discussed in the previous chapter world rugby is likely to be ever more characterized by diminishing contrasts as notions of 'sameness' become increasingly visible as migrant workers take their skills from country to country.

The number of players who represent a different country to the nation in which they were born remains one of the most contentious issues in international rugby. Of course place of birth is just one factor used in identifying eligibility requirements. As highlighted in Chapter 5 many scholars have looked at aspects of the migration of elite athletes and have contributed much to our understanding of how and why athletes move. For the most part these studies have focused on migration patterns and increasing numbers of migrant workers in various locales. What this work capably shows is that economics dictate migration flows and that athletes from poorer countries often move to wealthier nations.

One area that has received scant attention though is the conscious recruitment of overseas athletes to play for national teams. This is an issue not just of interest in rugby for a whole range of different sports include multiple cases of migration, issues surrounding eligibility and questions of what this means for the nation in the global arena. The focus on winning medals at major games and being successful in international tournaments now functions as a kind of 'Olympic arms race' (Green and Oakley, 2001). More and more money is spent on trying to achieve international sporting success and developing infrastructures to facilitate this. The Australian Institute of Sport (AIS) is often used as the model here given the remarkable success enjoyed by this nation in developing their sports systems following a dismal showing at the 1976 Olympic Games in Montreal (Stewart et al., 2004).

As the stakes become higher, and the pressure to win matches and trophies intensifies, shortcuts or anything to gain a competitive advantage are fair game in the contemporary rugby world. Many critics of professionalism highlight this 'win at all costs' mentality as being a particularly ugly side of the new (professional) rugby. Prior to open professionalism the game, in many ways, belonged to the players and was characterized as being very much a players' game (Horton, 2009). The 'Bloodgate' controversy, where the London club Harlequins, were found guilty of deliberately faking a blood injury in a Heineken Cup game against Leinster is probably the most high profile example of this in recent times. The spirit of rugby and the values that are supposed to be central to the game is still cited as a key aspect of the sport (IRB, 2008). Yet one area that has received relatively little attention here is the conscious recruitment of non-nationals to play for a national rugby team. This is particularly interesting when considered in light of the role of sport in serving as a particular identifier of 'the nation' and signifier of national pride (Bairner, 2009; Hope, 2002; Jarvie and Walker, 1994).

'Grannygate' and labour migration

Whereas some players moved to play their sport in another country and settled there by virtue of marriage or developing a particular affinity for the place, in an age of increased migration others are consciously recruited to represent a national team. One of the key moments that led to a tightening in the regulations concerning international representation surrounded events commonly referred to as 'Grannygate'. David Hilton who was born in Bristol played his club rugby for the very successful Bath team in England but represented the Scottish national team 41 times on the basis that his paternal grandfather was born in Edinburgh. It transpired that his grandfather was also born in Bristol and so the 'root' of Hilton's eligibility was a false one. Hilton had first represented Scotland in the amateur era and the President of the Scottish Rugby Union claimed in an article in *The Independent* (20 March 2000) that there should be a distinction between eligibility requirements:

> In our submission to the IRB we are suggesting that the point at which the game became open in August 1995 should be the cut-off as far as stringent adherence to the eligibility regulations is concerned. Any players who committed themselves to a Union's cause as amateurs prior to that date who can demonstrate that they did not deliberately flout eligibility rules, should be permitted to continue to represent their country.

Part of the issue here seems to point to the fact that the professional game was much more open to exploitation and a bending of the rules representing a noticeable shift from the values that the sport was built upon. Hilton's mistake was an honest one and he signed an affidavit to confirm that he genuinely believed his grandfather was born in Edinburgh. The fact that his 'eligibility', like that of other players with more dubious claims, had not ever been checked points to some of the practices commonplace in rugby at the time.

The 'Granny rule' had been a feature of Jack Charlton's reign as manager of the Republic of Ireland football team (Ticher, 1994). Under Charlton the country qualified for world cup finals and made significant progress in the international arena bringing a newfound popularity to the sport in the emerald isle. Yet of course this did not occur in isolation and was 'interwoven with social and cultural developments in contemporary Ireland' (Bairner, 2001: p. 88). Consciously recruiting players born outside the country became a key feature of rugby in the professional era. While this had always happened in the amateur game with the advent of professionalism this became a more strategic initiative on the part of many unions and also reflected the increasing internationalization of the sport within and between certain nations.

The signing of Iestyn Harris from Leeds RL is probably the most high profile example of this in Wales but Harris had represented Wales in rugby league. Moreover his signing was seen by many to be something of a payback given that it was only due to the fact that his grandfather had been tempted to England in the first place that led to Harris being born and raised in England (Harris, 2006). More controversial was the costly recruitment of Jason Jones-Hughes from Australia. Also of Welsh descent Jones-Hughes had represented Australia A and Under 21s. Initially it was ruled that as he had represented Australia A, he had made a commitment to them but this decision was overturned and he represented Wales in the 1999 Rugby World Cup. Many commentators trace the demise of Graham Henry's reign as Welsh coach to the 'Grannygate' controversy. Fellow New Zealanders Brett Sinkinson and Shane Howarth had been tempted to Wales by Henry and both represented the national team on the basis that each had a Welsh grandparent. Nobody from the WRU had checked these claims and although both players made important contributions to the team it later transpired that neither had a Welsh grandparent and so were not eligible to play for Wales. Soon the make-up of the Welsh team became cannon fodder for a number of people and Johnson (2000: p. 204) noted that 'qualification appeared to be based around being able to produce an old theatre stub as proof of having attended Max Boyce's Christmas pantomime'. Former players have expressed their discomfort with the fact that non-nationals represent their country. Allan Bateman (2001: p. 112) noted:

> Nationality is important to me at international level, and I disagreed with Henry when he introduced foreigners into the Wales squad soon after his arrival. I could understand his thinking but you should not pick and choose when it comes to a country and it was natural justice of sorts when Henry found himself caught up in an eligibility scandal during the 2000 Six Nations.

Adrian Hadley (2001: p. 173) also expressed similar views when discussing Shane Howarth's part in 'Grannygate':

> [E]ven though I got on well with Shane and admired him as a player, it didn't sit too easily on my shoulders as a Welshman to see him pulling on the famous red jersey. Nothing personal but Shane wasn't Welsh by birth. It's as simple as that. It pisses me off that players can chop and change their allegiance to countries.

These events led to a change in the IRB regulations whereby there is now a tighter control on player eligibility and once someone has received representative honours at senior level for a national team, the next senior fifteen A-side team or the national Sevens team, then he is not eligible to play for any other country. Throughout the rugby world there are numerous cases of players being recruited to represent another country to that within which they were born. Much controversy has long since surrounded the recruitment of Pacific Islanders to play for the national teams of New Zealand and Australia (see especially, Dewey, 2008; Grainger, 2006) and it is to this subject that I now turn.

Overstayers and kilted Kiwis: The new age of professionalism

The links between New Zealand, Australia and certain Pacific Islands deserve particular attention here as this remains one of the most contentious and controversial subjects in the world of international rugby. New Zealand and Australia are frequently accused of pillaging these islands and taking away all of the best players. The national teams of these respective nations feature luminaries such as Viliami Ofahengaue and Jerry Collins who were born outside the shores of the nation they represented. The New Zealand squad for the 2007 world cup finals featured eight players born outside the country. Of these there were five from Samoa, two from Fiji and one from Tonga clearly highlighting the lines of migration into New Zealand rugby. Yet it should also be noted that Fiji and Tonga each comprised one player born outside their respective borders (and in each case it was a New Zealander) but little was mentioned about the five Tongans in the US squad. An interesting case is presented when looking at the Samoan squad for this championship which included 14 New Zealand–born players among their number.

Grainger (2006) outlines the relationship between Samoa and New Zealand and explores the discursive space between them (see also, Dewey, 2008). In the professional age of rugby the pressure to move because of the economic incentives accentuates this relationship between core and periphery. While immigrants may be the subject of restrictions and oppression, the rules often change when it involves elite athletes and the sports world is replete with examples of athletes receiving special treatment at the hands of governments. For those moving from the Pacific Islands a period of residency then means that the individual will be eligible to represent the country they have settled in as long as they have no representative honours in their home country. Some commentators in the Pacific Islands have accused the bigger rugby nations of deliberately issuing young players with international honours, even in the Sevens game, to ensure that they then have to commit themselves to that nation. Teaiwa and Mallon (2005) have also explored the relationship between New Zealand and the Pacific Islands noting the stereotypes attached to Polynesian people and their lack of rugby nous. The front cover of the New Zealand edition of *Rugby World* magazine (October, 2001) asked, 'Where Have all the White Players Gone?' and explored some of the tensions in the country. Tana Umaga became the first person of Pacific Island ancestry to captain the All Blacks in 2004 and carefully positioned himself as a New Zealander of Samoan parentage, who is proud of his culture and his parents' background, but is 'a New Zealander first and foremost' (quoted in *Sunday Star Times*, 6 February 2005). Grainger's (2006) analysis adds much to the literature on migration in sport. This work is valuable for locating the migration of rugby players within a series of wider socio-historical relationships and examines how the players negotiate an identity 'simultaneously informed by colonial legacy, notions of "homeland", and the economic demands of global capitalism' (Grainger, 2006: p. 46).

It is clear that the cases of national representation are much more complex than often presented and some nations have much closer links than others leading to a greater flow of people between these places and a more established relationship. While even the most severe critic of the All Blacks would acknowledge that some of the players born outside the country have very close ties to the nation, this is not always the case in other nations. To further explore the subject of non-nationals representing a particular team I briefly look at Scotland as an example of another nation that has an interesting history of inward migration in the professional game.

Jim Telfer (2005: p. 253) reflected on the challenges he faced when coaching Scotland in the increasingly competitive world of international rugby:

> The selectors had witnessed how difficult it was becoming for Scottish teams to compete at world level, so we turned our attention to Scottish-qualified players outside Scotland, men whose parents or grandparents were born here. It was not new, but a route taken for over a century in Scottish rugby; and in the late

1980s, with a shortage of big, strong forwards in our game, we went to England to uncover new talent.

As the challenges brought about by professionalism intensified Telfer (2005) noted that now they were receiving information from agents about certain players and a sizeable number of Scottish-qualified New Zealanders in particular. Two sons of All Blacks legend Andy Leslie played for the Scotland national team. John and Martin Leslie were to become important figures in the Scotland team and were part of a core group of men from New Zealand who newspapers at the time described as the 'kilted kiwis'. Their representing Scotland caused much controversy particularly with the case of Brendan Laney who first pulled on a representative jersey just four days after arriving in the country. Telfer (2005) noted that while he would have loved to see the whole match-day squad of 22 born in the country 'it was as plain as the noses on our faces that the rest of the top-tier nations were moving ahead of us and we had to find something extra' (p. 255).

As is the case with New Zealand coaches appearing all over the rugby world there are also numerous other New Zealanders representing different nations. Some like Jamie Joseph, previously capped by the All Blacks, represented the Japanese national team. His countryman Andrew McCormick went on to be the first foreigner to captain the national side and lead them in the 1999 World Cup. Light, Hirai and Ebishima (2008: p. 147) note that the increase in foreign players 'is particularly noticeable in the number of non-Japanese players in the national team, and, as we have suggested, this has deflected from the traditional cultural meaning of rugby in Japan' (see also, Sakata, 2004). Sakata (2004) notes how in the 2003–4 season 14 full internationals from the Pacific Islands were represented in a Top League team in the country. Increasingly we may witness more and more younger players recruited from these islands to enter Japan for a university degree or a post with one of the big teams and thus become eligible for the Japanese team. Sakata (2004) notes that players from the Pacific Islands are generally less expensive than those from New Zealand and this will be an interesting development to track as Japan aims to make its presence felt as it hosts the 2019 world cup.

As Ticher (1994: p. 75) has noted there are 'an increasing number of international players, across a whole range of sports, whose apparently "obvious" nationality conflicts with the country they represent'. An article on the scrum.com website (23 February 2009) suggested that nothing has been more damaging to the reputation of the international game than the sight of players representing nations they had no obvious connections to (such as New Zealanders Jamie Joseph with Japan, Tony Marsh for France and Shane Howarth with Wales).

There are numerous other cases where players actively seek (or are sought out by national unions) international honours by representing a country they have little or no affiliation to. Given its history as a colonial outpost and important financial centre the Hong Kong team has often comprised a number of different nationalities in its national side. The small Mediterranean island of Malta has fielded an international rugby team since 1995 and due to the very small number of players there they have awarded international honours to players of Maltese descent from very low levels of the British amateur game. This of course represents a very different case to that of the Russian team who qualified for the 2003 world cup finals but was later expelled from the tournament following complaints about the eligibility of three South African players in their team.

Roots, routes and birth certificates

At the 2007 World Cup finals 98 players on the rosters of national teams were born outside of the country they were representing in the tournament. The bare statistics only tell part of the tale though. Ronan O'Gara, for example, has an Irish name and speaks in a distinctly Irish accent. He was schooled in Ireland and plays for the Munster province. Yet due to his father's work O'Gara was actually born in the US so could have represented that country. This example is a markedly different case than that of Budge Poutney who represented Scotland with distinction for many years by virtue of a grandmother born in the Channel Islands off the south coast of England! Having previously represented England at Under 21 level this family connection made Poutney eligible for all of the home nations. An abrasive flanker, Poutney captained the national side and was referred to as a 'braveheart' by the Edinburgh-based *Edinburgh Evening News* (7 April 1999). He retired from international rugby at the age of 29 accusing the Scottish Rugby Union of 'unprofessionalism' and treating their players badly. *The Independent* (5 November 2000) described the player as 'more Bergerac than Braveheart by virtue of the Channel Islands-born grandmother who gave him his Scottish qualification' highlighting the ways in which media narratives can be framed both to make non-nationals key signifiers of the nation or conversely highlight quite clearly that they are different or the 'other' in some discourse.

Part of the problem with developing typologies and adhering to one theoretical 'badge' in trying to explain migration patterns is that it tends to generalize from a relatively small number of cases. An obvious outcome of increased commercialism is that as the rewards became bigger competing nations would look to every possible avenue to gain a competitive advantage. It would also be safe to assume that as the professional age witnessed an increase in migration between nations and a widening of the recruitment net we would witness more and more diverse national teams. Yet it is also important to note that throughout the history of the game there are cases of players being selected for nations other than that in which they were born and/or had lived for most of their lives although national eligibility was much less of a concern than whether the player was really an amateur in the period up to 1995.

What open professionalism and increased globalization facilitated was an intensification of these movements both in terms of planned recruitment by nations but also through national eligibility occurring as an unintended result of professional migration. As the commercial aspects of the game became more significant the results on the field of play mattered much more and so any attempt to gain an advantage was seized upon. What we also saw in some places was the implementation of strategic initiatives aimed at deliberately targeting individuals from a particular nation to strengthen the playing resources in another country.

The complex and changing dynamic of the rugby world was shown when Lesley Vainikolo was selected to play for the England national (union) team. Vainikolo, who had joined Gloucester RFC after five successful years in English rugby league with Bradford Bulls, was born in Tonga and represented New Zealand in rugby league. As a rugby union player, with no prior representative experience, he could have chosen to play for the country of his birth (Tonga), his parents' birthplace (New Zealand) or the country he had resided in for over five years (England). Henry Paul had also represented New Zealand in rugby league but played for England in rugby union due to an English grandfather and a cross-code transfer supported by the Rugby Football Union. The cost of recruiting converts such as Paul proved to be a highly contentious issue. As outlined in Chapter 3 throughout much of the rugby world many expensive league converts failed to adapt to the union game and some were to return to the thirteen-man game having made little impact in their new sport. As also highlighted in Chapter 3, despite visions of a hybrid game and/ or year round rugby players, the two sports remained very different and it was not an easy transition from one to the other.

So with the increase in non-national players and coaches across the game, and as we each become more similar through globalization processes, it was suggested that the importance of the nation would decline. If anything, in certain cultural contexts, we have seen an increase in the stated importance of the nation. Sport in particular continues to be a significant site where 'the nation' does matter. In nations that may be marginalized in a range of other spheres the international sporting stage represents an important place to promote and celebrate nationhood. Globalization continues to have a major impact upon our understanding of national cultures and identities but as Bairner (2001: p. 163) has noted 'nationalism coexists alongside globalisation and is at times strengthened by it'. Despite globalization's impact upon economies, societies and cultural processes, it is imperative to note that notions of nationality and national identity have retained their importance (Edensor, 2002). To represent one's country in rugby remains a schoolboy dream for many players and some may turn down the chance of playing for a more established nation in order to pursue that dream. Yet for others economic factors dictate that they may have to commit to another jersey early on in their career even if they do not feel any sense of belonging in that colour shirt.

Interestingly, from a number of newspaper articles at the time of 'Grannygate' there seemed to be more angst and concern that 'foreigners' could be eligible to play for the British and Irish Lions than there was for the make-up of the national squads of the respective home nations. The subject of British identity represents a particularly pertinent case to consider for this is something that in general terms has declined markedly in recent years. So while rugby players represent one of the four home nations the sport also affords the very best of them the opportunity to represent a combined British and Irish team every four years.

8

The Lions Roar: British Identity and the Professional Game

In relation to national identities of contemporary times rugby provides us with an interesting scenario that is not present in many other sports. While the four home unions play each other annually in the Six Nations championships they also come together once every four years to form the British and Irish Lions. On a calendar that incorporates quadrennial trips to South Africa, Australia and New Zealand (with the next tour scheduled for Australia in 2013) this provides players from the home unions a chance to challenge some of the leading powers in the sport in their own backyard. In itself this is a testing and daunting task yet for the Lions this is something undertaken on very limited preparation time all the while trying to meld individuals from four very different cultures. Carwyn James, coach of the victorious 1971 Lions, prepared his team with the following speech:

> First and foremost, it is imperative that you be your own man. I want you to be not as you are perceived in your office, but as in your own home. I don't want you Irish to pretend to be English, or English to be Celts, or Scotsmen to be anything less than Scots. Yet Scots must make bosom buddies of Englishmen, Irish of Welshmen, everybody of everybody – yet at the same time the Irish must remain ideologists off the field and on it fighters like Kilkenny cats; the English must keep their stiff upper lips and just be superior, the Scots be dour as well as radical, and the Welsh continue to be as bloody-minded as their history demands.

While not underplaying the marvellous achievements of earlier Lions teams, like the one coached by James, in the professional age the challenge may be conceived as even bigger given that the opposition would now be professional units used to training together for significant periods of time every year. While the Lions players might also be professionals they would not have this time together as a group and so would seem to be at a serious disadvantage when compared to their opponents. Yet the lure of playing for the Lions remains one of the most sought after honours in the game and this is still something that most British and Irish rugby players aspire to. Perhaps the most important figure associated with the Lions in the professional era Ian McGeechan, Head Coach of the 1997 and 2009 Lions, summed it up best when he noted that the Lions team represents four nations coming together as one, that the Lions were about the legends who had worn the famous red jersey and that those presented with the opportunity to wear the shirt could become legends themselves.

During the early days of professionalism, and the seemingly endless club versus country controversies and debates, many of the long-standing traditions of the game were perceived to be under threat. One of the most vulnerable of these, it was suggested, was the tour to the southern hemisphere of the British and Irish Lions. Tuck and Maguire (1999) noted that the changes to the game in the early years of professionalism meant that the existence of Lions tours was threatened by the expansion of European club competition. From the time of the first recorded tour at the end of the 1880s, which was not organized by the unions but by private promoters (Thomas, 2005), the Lions have become an important part of the international rugby world. Indeed given that a world cup competition did not start until 1987 it would be fair to state that they were arguably the most important link between northern and southern hemisphere rugby. The first touring team was actually a predominantly English one and their expedition took them away from home for a little over eight months. Just 22 players made up the touring party who played a total of 53 games. More than a century on and Sir Clive Woodward's 2005 Lions, with double the amount of players, were away for less than a quarter of this time and played 11 games. In fact the 2005 Lions party included more support staff (coaches, masseurs, analysts) than there were players on the 1888 tour! Of course this reflects not just the impact of professionalism but also the increased commercialization and commodification of the game where the demands of the clubs and national unions see to it that players are not away with the Lions for too long. Alongside the changes to rugby it is also important to note the changing conceptions of what it means to be British. The next section considers some of the most pertinent issues before reflecting on the four Lions tours of the professional era.

The changing face of Britain

It is a particularly interesting time to look at British identity given the many changes of recent years. As Weight (2002) notes at the beginning of his comprehensive tome on British national identity from 1940–2000 the country 'did change dramatically in this period' (p. 1) and many people stopped considering themselves British. Yet parts of British society still seem subsumed by references to an imperial past when 'Britannia ruled the waves' and the country was conceived as truly 'Great'. Much of this is usually couched in terms of militaristic terminology with reference to England and is particularly prevalent during major sporting competitions and most notably international football tournaments (e.g. Crolley and Hand, 2002; Garland and Rowe, 1999; Harris, 1999; Weed, 2001). In the mid-1990s attempts to 'modernize' and move towards a 'Cool Britannia', a renewal of vigour in the lifeblood of the nation, was often interpreted as a shift away from ideologies underpinned by 'Rule Britannia'. Cannadine (2003) argues that 'Cool Britannia' was no replacement for 'Rule Britannia' and indeed 'Cool Britannia' was to become a much-maligned term and seen as part of a Blairite attempt to rebrand things where 'spin' rather than substance became a staple part of media communications. Blair's so called 'spin doctor' Alistair Campbell will be looked at later in this chapter in relation to his involvement with the 2005 British and Irish Lions.

Massive changes to the population itself also reshaped the country – most notably through the inward migration of peoples from former colonies. While space does not permit a detailed discussion of these issues here, it is important to note that in the period since 1945 the racial make-up of the country changed dramatically. Scholars have looked at many of the most important issues in relation to sport (e.g. Burdsey, 2008; Carrington and McDonald, 2001; Cashmore,

1982). Again though, I find that while much of this may be couched in 'British' terms the issues discussed in many texts are largely about England where, it must also be acknowledged, the vast percentage of black and Asian immigrants settled. I will return to issues concerning race in British rugby shortly but first consider some of the other significant changes impacting upon British identity.

The contested and contentious relationship between England and the Celtic fringe is best highlighted with reference to devolution. A key marker in the late 1990s, and important when looking at the increased affiliation with a national identity that is not British, these events are often positioned as important markers in the independence of England's smaller neighbours although it must be noted that the actual significance of this change differs from country to country. Collectively what this has influenced is a sharp downward trend in the number of people now identifying themselves as British (Rojek, 2007; Weight, 2002).

An even more recent concern has seen an acceleration of the post-imperial decline of the country to the extent that Great Britain is no longer seen as a proud and upstanding nation and instead has been replaced by a *Little Britain*. The popular comedy show of this name portrays a nation that Rojek (2007: p. 12) notes is a 'moronic inferno of welfare state scroungers, terraced-house-dwelling bigots, corrupt leaders, gullible consumers, indignant victims, fat trolls and shrill jobsworths'. While it may be a comedy-sketch-show, part of its popularity, as with other contemporary comedies such as *The Office* and *Gavin and Stacey*, is that it reflects and parodies real situations and people that many of us can relate to. A popular newspaper, in response to many of the widespread social ills, has taken to referring to 'Broken Britain' and it regularly frames stories within a narrative of a country in a state of seemingly terminal decline.

The above clearly shows some of the important issues omnipresent when looking at aspects of British identity in contemporary times. In addition to the points outlined previously we must also not neglect the importance of Europeanization discourse and what is often perceived as a threat to British national identity (Weight, 2002). Britain has demonstrated a strong resistance to European integration, partly as a result of its geographical locatedness as an island and also as a reflection of a continued suspicion and distrust of the 'other'. English football teams still talk of getting into

Europe (see Millward, 2006; Williams and Wagg, 1991) and despite the noticeable internationalization of the sport (e.g. Lanfranchi and Taylor, 2001; McGovern, 2002) there continues to be some suspicion of foreigners and notions of difference within the game. Rugby has also engaged, albeit in limited ways, with Europeanization as evidenced by the hugely successful European rugby competitions that have taken place since 1995. The addition of Italy to the Five Nations championships in 2000 may also be used as reflective of the increased Europeanization of the game yet they remain very much on the periphery of the sport and are yet to mount a serious challenge for the title. The increase in the number of overseas players in domestic rugby competitions has previously been discussed (see Chapter 5) but it is also important to note here that freedom of movement under European constitutional law means that citizens of EU member states are free to live and pursue employment across national borders. To date this has been less of an issue for British rugby than some other sports because of the fact that the game is not particularly popular in many European nations.

To the best of my knowledge it is only recently that reference to a team by the name of the British and Irish Lions has been widely visible though it should be noted that the last two touring parties have been captained by men from the South of Ireland. Yet it is still the British Lions that most rugby fans and commentators refer to when discussing the team. While acknowledging and not wishing to underplay the importance of Irish players and coaches within the Lions this chapter focuses predominantly on British identity, the interplay of English, Scottish and Welsh identities and the place of the touring team in the professional rugby world.

England as Britain: Britain as England

The very concept of a British identity remains a somewhat thorny issue and the challenge of melding patriotism in a poly-ethnic and increasingly internationalized society is a particularly tough one. Holt (1989) notes how Englishness was rarely understood by foreigners 'for whom "England", "Britain", and the "United Kingdom" were obstinately synonomous' (p. 237). The use of the terms 'Britain' and 'England', interchangeably and with little recognition of their inherent differences, is sure to annoy those from the Celtic fringe.

Academia is certainly no different in this respect and numerous books and articles titled with Britain focus largely (or sometimes exclusively) on England. The sports literature is replete with examples that do this often unknowingly promoting an Anglo-centric focus that over-simplifies and collapses many of the key differences between its various parts.

Rugby rarely receives a mention in any broader texts on British identities and cultures. Even the most insightful books about sport in British society touch on the Lions sparingly. Holt's (1989) work includes a passing mention to the team while a cursory look at the index of Polley's (1998) text shows two brief entries on the team (half of that afforded to just one football player, Paul 'Gazza' Gascgoine). Yet by and large many texts on British sports are focused on the constituent parts and the differences between nations. This is not meant as a criticism of such work for the texts identified above do much to clearly articulate the differences between, for example, rugby in Wales compared to rugby in England. I make this point to highlight that more work is needed in exploring wider *British* identities in sport.

Tuck's (1996) research is very useful in exploring how a range of national playing styles is portrayed. Based on historical research he identifies dominant narratives from *The Times* newspaper where the Welsh are 'magical, wild and creative', the Scottish are 'fanatical, fiery and courageous', the Irish may be 'tigerish, violent and marauding' and the English are characterized as 'gentlemanly, orderly and honest' (p. 34). The players themselves offer interesting views on the other nations where of course it is the English who remain the biggest enemy for many players from the Celtic nations (Tuck and Maguire, 1999).

As indicated earlier, the challenge for the Lions is to meld these disparate groups together. This team sport represents a very different scenario than say the Great Britain athletics squad for even when competing in major events athletics is still largely an individual sport and competitors perform in the same way. In rugby, a hard physical contact sport, players engage in head-to-head combat. As the game became more professionalized it was noticeable that the sport had become markedly faster and the tackles much harder (Bathgate et al., 2002; Malcolm and Sheard, 2002). This was a reflection of the fact that as full-time athletes the players now devoted themselves exclusively to the sport and did not have to fit training sessions around their day jobs. Many Englishmen on the 2001 Lions tour felt that they were doing things with England that was much better than what they were experiencing on tour. Players from the other nations noted that in terms of their physical conditioning and all-round preparation England were way ahead of the Celtic nations (e.g. Williams, 2009). Part of the challenge in developing a successful Lions tour is to be able to put national issues/rivalries to one side and avoid the formation of cliques whereby players only mix with others from their home nation. The next section looks at some of the issues and events that have helped shape perceptions and understanding of the Lions in the professional era with a particular focus on issues relating to the nation and national identities.

The Lions and professional rugby: 1997–2009

Of course the challenge of melding individuals from different teams and divergent cultures has always been a tricky one. In the days of amateurism, save for the Five Nations and mid-week Anglo-Welsh matches, players were rarely in contact with their contemporaries from the other home nations. This would have changed as a result of professionalism where now more of the players would cross borders to earn a living and the introduction of European cup competitions meant that teams from the four unions played each other much more often. In the professional age, where the quality of the opposition also improved significantly, the tour represents an even bigger challenge for the team to be able to compete with the leading southern hemisphere nations. England had proven quite capable of doing this on its own under the direction of Clive Woodward although some of the main issues surrounding the 2001 and 2005 tours were related to this very issue (Butler, 2001; Carter, 2008). In 2001, despite England being the best team in the Six Nations, Woodward was overlooked for the Lions' post that went to Graham Henry. This according to many reports caused an uneasy relationship between Woodward and Henry. Alun Carter, notational analyst on the 2001 tour, noted that Woodward seemed to associate more with the Australian management team during the tour in what was perceived as a very public snub to the Lions (Carter, 2008). Throughout the history of the Lions there was often a recognition of a need to be inclusive, to be wary of the sensibilities of all nations and not feature too many players from just the one country. In the professional age though the focus is more about results on the field of play and less about appeasing a certain faction. Since their victorious first tour of the openly professional era, to South Africa in 1997, the British and Irish Lions have failed to win a test series. The successes of 1997 were attributed in part to the 'professional' attitude that league converts Allan Bateman, John Bentley, Scott Gibbs, Scott Quinnell, Alan Tait and Dai Young brought with them. Yet the tour still had links to the amateur era and many refer to it as their greatest rugby experience (e.g. Dallaglio, 2007). Screened on *Sky Sports* the 1997 Lions were promoted in a way not seen before and their performances did much to raise the profile of the sport. The squad was successful as all players genuinely felt they had a chance of competing for a place in the test-match squad and the coaching team went with the form players and were not afraid to make tough decisions.

Somewhat controversially, Graham Henry was selected as Head Coach of the Lions for the 2001 tour to Australia. Many were annoyed by the decision to appoint Henry as he was not British. In fact as numerous players who appeared on that tour noted perhaps it was because he was an outsider that he did not understand the tradition of the Lions and what it was meant to symbolize. His widely repeated words that 'In this part of the world, they don't respect you. They don't think you're good enough. They don't think you're fit enough, they don't think you're skilful enough and they don't think you're strong enough. And I should know because I'm one of them' (cited in Dallaglio, 2007: p. 377) was more an unfortunate choice of wording than an observation on the state of British rugby. Much of the discontent from this tour, and the controversial newspaper columns of two members of the touring party (England's Austin Healey and Matt Dawson), surrounded the lack of any free time and the monotony of preparation for matches. Even the popular Jason Leonard, a man rarely associated with negative comments and known to all in the game as 'the fun bus', commented on seeing two other countries during his time as a British Lion but not seeing anything of Australia (Leonard, 2004). Butler (2001) perceptively noted that while the word professional may have featured in the mission statement as a positive adjective it 'became the single word that would explain away any harshness' (p. 23). The great challenge for those leading the Lions is not only in bringing together players from different nations but also ensuring that the touring party as a whole is cohesive and that it does not separate into two distinct factions of the test team and the rest. Previous Lions tours had suffered when players who felt they had no chance of selection for the test matches went 'off tour' and some returned home considerably heavier than when they left the Isles. In 2001 many players felt that the test team had been selected before the party departed (see for example, Healey, 2006; Williams, 2009) and this issue was also to be a key factor during the following tour.

By the time of the next tour Henry was back home in New Zealand and in position as the All Blacks coach ready to welcome the 2005 Lions when Clive Woodward finally ascended to the position he craved so much in 2001. Working with Henry were Steve Hansen and Wayne Smith, both of whom had substantial experience of the British game having each spent time in coaching positions on the Isles before returning to work with the New Zealand squad. The criticism labeled at Henry that as a foreigner he fell short for not understanding the ethos of the Lions was not something that could be directed at the Englishman Woodward who had toured with the Lions as a player in the early 1980s. Yet in many ways Woodward threatened the underpinning traditions and the very concept of the Lions more than Henry. His decision to tour with a squad of 44 players and a backroom staff of 26 upset and confused many traditionalists. The idea to go with a much larger squad was linked to the increased number of injuries in the professional era. As players became bigger and stronger the injury rates did see an increase (Bathgate et al., 2002); although as Malcolm and Sheard (2002) note, in the professional game the medical attention and support afforded to players also improved dramatically (see also, Malcolm, 2006). England had won the world cup two years earlier but many felt that Woodward was still selecting players based on what they had achieved in 2003. Some of the Celtic players felt isolated and that the test team had been picked before they had left the Isles (see for example, Henson, 2005; Williams, 2009).

In 2009 under the leadership of Lions stalwart Ian McGeechan, assisted by a coaching team that included the New Zealand-born Warren Gatland, the Lions returned to South Africa. As noted in Chapter 6, Gatland had coached the Irish national team and London Wasps before leading Wales to a Grand Slam in 2008. As he was not the Head Coach there was less controversy than there had been when

Henry was appointed. Matt Stevens had a very strong chance of being in the touring party and facing the country of his birth before his well-documented suspension for failing a drugs test. During the 2009 tour another landmark in the increased globalization of the sport was reached when Riki Flutey became the first man to play against and then subsequently for the Lions. Flutey had faced the Lions in 2005 as a member of the Wellington team. By 2009 he was an established England international, having qualified to play for the country on residency grounds, and an important member of the British and Irish Lions squad.

The challenge to make a true unified team has often been beset by political issues and various national agendas over the years. At different times certain nations have dominated the game with choices of coach and captain sometimes being controversial ones. England have been the dominant force among the home nations in the professional era so it is no surprise that they have also contributed the most players to the touring parties in the four professional tours to date. Scotland's sometime abject performances and struggles with professionalism are reflected by the fact that they have contributed by far the least number of players to the Lions since 1997. For the first test in South Africa in 2009, there was no Scottish player in the match-day squad whereas 20 years earlier there were two from just the one Scottish family in the starting 15. Of course this percentage of players from the different nations may also be reflective of the success of the respective national teams so that Ireland, fresh from completing their first Grand Slam in 60 years, had more players selected in the original 2009 touring party of 37 than any other nation. This was the first time since the game went professional that England was not the country with the most players in a Lions squad.

To further consider the changes that open professionalism brought it is interesting to note that during the last Lions tour of the amateur era in 1993 apart from two Scottish internationals who played for London Scottish only one other player (Andy Reed) played his club rugby outside of the country he represented. The first tour of the professional era, in 1997, featured eight players playing their club rugby outside of their home nation (nine if you include the Irish international playing for London Irish). All of these eight players were earning a living in England hereby demonstrating the rapid emergence of that country as an economic force in the sport. For as indicated previously with its larger playing base and greater financial resources England were much better placed than the other home unions to support professional rugby. Fewer Lions players have played outside their home nation at the time of selection in recent tours but it will be interesting to see how many of the 2013 Lions are playing their club rugby in France.

As noted earlier Britishness is often conflated with Englishness and the hegemony of the English nation. Collins (2009) notes how Britishness was often perceived as a subordinate sub-set of Englishness for both those who governed rugby and for English society in general. Yet while England may have dominated notions of British identity in the majority of spheres the Lions became an important symbol of all the constituent parts. The great success and impressive performances by players such as Barry John, Gavin Hastings and Willie John McBride showed that all of the four unions were integral to the Lions. Here then, in the rugby playing nations of the world at least, there was a clear recognition and understanding that Britain and England were two different things. This in itself is significant for in many other places the two terms are used interchangeably with little acknowledgement (or awareness) of the differences between the two. When a group of Scottish women, representing Great Britain, won a gold medal for curling in the 2002 Olympic Games, the screen at the arena referred to them as England during one of the earlier stages of the competition.

Throngs of Welsh supporters wearing British Lions jerseys are a staple feature of Lions tours (see for example, Nicholls, 2006). The prevalence of Welsh flags where the red dragon appears alongside the name of a local rugby club points to the multi-dimensional nature of identities. Although supporting a Britain and Ireland team, including a number of players from their most hated foe, England, these supporters retain a strong Welsh identity. Many England players have written about the hatred and hostility they have faced from Welsh fans (e.g. Greenwood, 2005; Healey, 2005; Leonard, 2004) yet these same players would be cheered on by Welshmen and women when wearing the red shirt of the Lions. Moreover the display of a flag bearing the name of a particular rugby club or town, motivated of course in part by the desire to be seen back home, also points to a powerful local affiliation and particular sense of place. To this end local pride is also celebrated alongside a Welsh national identity and a British one. Temporarily at least the English players who for most of the time are the sworn enemy are now part of a collective 'us' as New Zealand, South Africa or Australia become 'them'. Of course local pride in Welsh rugby is even more pertinent considering that two of the most storied and fanatical towns in the game, Bridgend and Pontypridd, lost their top-level teams during the process of regionalization and then subsequently also lost their regional franchise with the early demise of the Celtic Warriors.

Race, ethnicity and the Lions

It is also important to note that the Lions always were, and continue to remain, very much a white team. Since the advent of professionalism only a very small number of ethnic minorities have represented the Lions. Jeremy Guscott and Tony Underwood, both of mixed-race parentage, were part of the 1997 squad while rugby league convert Jason Robinson was selected in 2001 and 2005. The only non-white player from the other nations who has represented the touring team in the professional era is former Welsh captain Colin Charvis who was part of Graham Henry's 2001 Lions. Charvis is also the only forward among this group of players but it is also important to note that he was actually born and raised in England. I highlight this for in the context of recognizing the racial and ethnic changes to the country it is important to note that England is very different from the Celtic nations. Within a few years it is suggested that there will be more children born in Britain (England?) with the surnames Singh or Patel than there will be Smith, Williams or Brown (all names of former Lions players). The Office of National Statistics data shows that Mohammed (and other names with similar spellings such as Muhammed) is now the third most popular name for boys born in England (*Daily Mail*, 11 September 2009). Former foreign secretary Robin Cooke suggested that chicken tikka masala has surpassed fish and chips as the 'national dish' although again this is a disputed area and there are also strong claims that each nation within Britain has its own national dish. The team that ran onto the field for the first test of the 2009 series against South Africa featured just one non-white player in Harlequins and England wing Ugo Monye. The only other person in the 2009 squad who could be considered an ethnic minority was New Zealand–born Riki Flutey who is of Maori descent. If we include members of the coaching staff in the totals then more individuals born outside Britain have been involved with the Lions in the professional era than there have been British born ethnic minorities.

When compared to the British athletics team of the same period we can clearly see that in terms of its racial and ethnic diversity rugby seems to more closely resemble an older Britain. Because of rugby's position in England class-related ideologies are also sometimes used here to explain the whiteness of England and/or Lions teams although the unproblematic coupling of race and social class needs to be analysed much further in relation to issues such as this. England cricket teams of recent years have been captained by men of Asian descent and also featured names such as Panesar, Ramprakash and Bopara. As the part of Britain with the greatest racial diversity it is also worth noting that the England football team now regularly comprises almost as many black players as it does white players in a typical starting 11.

There is some evidence to suggest that racial stereotyping continues to take place within the game. Wedderburn's (1989) research identified that blacks made up just 2 per cent of players in the top three rugby divisions in England but more than 60 per cent of these played on the wing. Interviewed on Sky Sports about the potential make-up of the 2009 Lions squad and the suggested inclusion of winger Delon Armitage, former England Coach Dick Best caused much controversy by suggesting that 'you've always got to have a coloured boy in the team'. Best had thought he had made this remark 'off-camera' but like the former football manager Ron Atkinson he was to learn to his cost that this wasn't the case. Quite whether the racial diversity of a Lions squad changes in the coming years remains to be seen and it will represent an interesting site to continue to look at the meanings of British identity as the nation changes significantly and at a remarkable pace.

The Lions: Tradition, change and the contemporary rugby world

For traditionalists and many concerned rugby people the Lions reached their nadir in 2005 when Woodward included one-time Labour party 'spin doctor' Alistair Campbell as part of an extensive and expensive support group. While many were uncomfortable with this decision, more were annoyed by the sight of Campbell in various

Lions clothing. Prince William also made a visit to the Lions camp. As Thomas (2005: p. 261) stated 'the invitation to Prince Williams to join the tour and wear a Lions tracksuit was sacrilegious and ridiculous'. For many Woodward's tenure was to signal the end of the Lions concept and threatened the very existence of the touring team.

McGeechan's 2009 Lions were celebrated for their 'back to basics' approach and for a return to the Lions ethos, yet the sheer brutality of the second test where five of the touring party ended up in hospital following a particularly bruising encounter with the Springboks highlighted the magnitude of the challenge. After losing the first two tests some newspapers questioned whether the Lions concept could continue in the professional era as it was no longer perceived to be a fair and equal competition. Victory in the third test and the financial windfall that hosting a Lions tour brings the host country will surely mean that they continue to tour and remain an important part of the rugby landscape for many years to come.

Of course when viewed in relation to the wider sphere of international rugby and the power relationships in the sport, it is important to note that the SANZAR deal in 1995 meant that the southern hemisphere nations were now less dependent on the financial windfall of a Lions tour. While it was the giants of southern hemisphere rugby and the formation of SANZAR that proved to be the catalyst to open professionalism, it is in England and France that the economic power currently lies (see also, Chapter 5). In commercial terms the Lions have become a powerful brand and one that is guaranteed to bring in significant revenues for the hosting union. Perhaps we should also consider then whether the Lions have any role to play in 'reaching out' and visiting other countries outside the dominant core. Quite whether the IRB can, or wish to, do this remains to be seen although of course from the perspective of clubs and national unions, concern over player burnout remains an issue.

The whole concept of the Lions was perceived as one of the institutions most under threat by rugby union's professionalization and the developing Europeanization of the game (e.g. Tuck and Maguire, 1999). Yet what actually happened was that the Lions developed significantly as a 'brand' and that the traditions it promoted and celebrated helped serve as a throwback to the amateur era and offered a powerful reaffirmation that in some ways the game was still the same. The last Lions team of the amateur era wore the famous red shirt carrying the badge of the four home unions and a small marker to signify the jersey manufacturer. The first professional tour featured playing jerseys emblazoned with the name of a sponsor across the chest and over time the visibility of the sponsor has increased markedly with all of the associated 'razzmatazz' that goes along with the much more overt commercialization of sport (Allison, 2005). It also offers an interesting arena for promotion of a British identity at a time when notions of Britain and the whole meaning of what it is to be British continues to change.

9

Flattening the Rugby World

My mum was born in Pontypool. 'Pooler' was one of the prominent forces in British rugby during the latter decades of amateurism. Under the leadership of Ray Prosser it built a fearsome reputation as a hard and uncompromising place to play. The qualities of the Pontypool pack reflected the town itself – tough, rugged and dour. These were hard men many of whom went rugby training after a day of physical labour. Like many surrounding areas by the dawn of the professional era the town was a visible symbol of post-industrial decline. Once an important marker in the local identity of the town, a little more than two decades after they hosted the 1984 Wallabies touring team, Pontypool RFC was put up for sale for one pound. I remember standing on the bank at Pontypool Park watching this Australian team. To say I actually watched the game is probably an exaggeration for the match was played in thick mist and the occasional glimpse of a Wallaby jersey or a brief sighting of a man in the red, white and black hoops of the home team was a rare occurrence. Just as rare an occurrence in the professional age are sightings of these touring teams at places like Pontypool Park. Now the leading southern hemisphere nations play a series of test matches against their northern hemisphere counterparts and matches against club sides or regional teams are few and far between. As noted in the previous chapter Lions touring teams also played fewer matches, in a shorter time period, than ever before and here also supporters were deprived of the chance of watching these top players. The chance to promote and assert local pride for many clubs was lost. The former Australia centre Jason Little noted that 'now teams fly in for a one-off Test and fly out. You see

133

nothing, meet no one' (in Edwards, 2003: p. 230). Those who had experienced touring in the amateur era lamented that this was one of the best things about the sport and a characteristic that made it a unique activity. In many instances isotonic drinks have replaced the barrels of beer and something very important seems to have disappeared from the game. Television of course plays a key part here and at the same time there is also concern over the number of matches players are being asked to play in any given season. With the leading powers scheduling tours between north and south the seasons are also becoming much longer and it is hard for many of the elite players to have the requisite rest and recovery periods they need for what is becoming an increasingly physical game (see Bathgate et al., 2002; Brooks et al., 2005; Malcolm, 2006).

The move to a regional playing structure in many countries, as a key step in the professional era, has had very mixed results in relation to what this has meant for local identities. Ireland adapted much better than Scotland where the battle for control between the clubs and the districts continues to define the sport in the latter. It is not just a simple local/global dichotomy that defines rugby because as discussed at various stages the dynamics are multi-layered and can encompass multiple identities. Obviously, as is the case with all international sport, the nation has loomed large in the discussion and analysis presented to date. The 'regional' will also warrant further analysis in the areas where this is now the elite part of the game. In England and France the clubs continue to remain important yet even here the professionalization of the game saw, and continues to see, power struggles between these clubs and their respective national unions. A key component of this is that each year the clubs face the threat of relegation from the top leagues and in England this led to some owners looking if they could invest in another club and/or merge with them to guarantee topflight rugby. The sad demise of Richmond RFC, the third oldest rugby club in the world, reflects this most poignantly.

When the game went professional many clubs, who were playing in dilapidated and rather spartan conditions, embarked on groundsharing agreements with professional football clubs. A number of these were situated miles away from where the rugby club had been based for a century or more. To all intents and purposes there is much evidence that place matters less and less in professional rugby and that leading clubs in many nations are less 'local' than they have ever been. When I watched Brive defeat Leicester to lift the European Cup in 1997 almost all of the Brive team were French players. At the start of the 2009–10 season Brive had 22 foreign players in their squad. However, it is important to be wary of generalizations here when discussing the demise of the local. The Bridgend team I had supported since I was a young boy merged with Pontypridd to become the Celtic Warriors, under the move to regional playing structures in Wales, but within a short period of time this team had ceased operations altogether. This then is obviously a markedly different case to Llanelli who added the moniker Scarlets on becoming one of the five regional teams but little else really changed.

The rugby world: Flat or spiky?

Thomas Friedman (2007) contends that the world is flat. As noted previously he has pointed to the fall of the Berlin Wall as an important marker in this 'flattening' of the world. The fall of rugby's own Berlin Wall also led to a flattening of the wider rugby landscape and, as discussed at various junctures, the union game has benefited a great deal from the input of former league players and coaches. In positioning a flatter world the relationship between 'rootedness' and the increasing focus on routes is also important. In rugby terms I suggested that the lexus is professionalism while the olive tree is amateurism. Here what Friedman (2000) has identified as the tension between the globalization system and the forces of culture, geography, tradition and community seem particularly pertinent when analysed within the context of rugby. The sport held on to its 'roots', those traditions and cultural norms that defined the game, far longer than most sports due to its continued adherence to the ideals of amateurism. The postmodern age of globalization (Robinson, 2007) was already well advanced when rugby union finally went openly professional and so the sport had to change quickly. Certainly a number of the examples used throughout this text highlight that the rugby world is in many ways much flatter than it has ever been before. Facilitated by the increased connectivity and interdependency of the various scapes (Appadurai, 1996; Tomlinson, 1999) then it is clear that the game has progressed in many ways. Yet as I have also been at pains to point out much of this continues to occur across rather narrow and established lines within and between a very small group of nations.

Conversely Richard Florida (2008) has put forward a powerful argument to suggest that rather than being flat the world is actually spiky. Here the hegemonic positioning of a few select cities is identified as central to the vast majority of global developments. Although the cities may not all be the same a similar observation could be made regarding rugby where the power base has changed little over the years and the important cities assume an increasingly hegemonic role (e.g. Harris, 2008; Hautboir and Charrier, 2009). Will Carling once infamously referred to English rugby as being governed by '57 old farts'. Indeed throughout much of the world rugby remains a sport ruled by 'blazered buffoons' who have done little to help develop the sport as an international game. Here status and prestige is the name of the game and decisions are made based on self-interest and preserving the status quo. Nothing reflects this more than the voting to decide who should host world cup competitions and in the past the core nations have been accused by Yoshiro Mori of the Japanese Rugby Football Union of 'passing the ball around their friends' (BBC Sport, 17 November 2005).

In fact the whole history of professional rugby and the attempts to increase the appeal of the sport is very much a tale of reactive governance. It was after all the threat of a 'rebel' world championship rugby competition in 1983 that speeded up the decision to host the inaugural world cup competition. The game went openly professional in 1995 because of a media battle for control of the rugby codes. Cynics might suggest that there has only been some attempt to 'reach out' to various nations at a time when the game was lobbying hard to become an Olympic sport. As the much travelled coaching guru George Simpkin noted, rugby needs to become an Olympic sport to really develop in China and that more should have been done by the international rugby community when state-sponsored sport programmes in eastern European nations such as Romania and Georgia could have really developed the game in these places. The vested interests of the few are protected and the needs of the wider international rugby community are largely ignored. Perhaps like in football it will take a fundamental shift and a power struggle for the leadership of the game to lead to a further flattening of the rugby world.

The case of Argentina provides a most pertinent and visible example here to highlight the challenges for a nation positioned outside the core. As discussed earlier they have developed on the field of play despite, rather than as a result of, the established order of things and need support if this development is to continue. Argentina's plight is in some ways similar to that of Romania in the 1980s. During this period the Romanians showed themselves to be more than capable of matching many of the foundation unions on the field of play. An invitation to join the Five Nations would not have only contributed to the development on the playing side but also made a massive impact upon the financial position of the Romanian national team and the sport in that country as a whole. Yet these claims were ignored and the revolution in that country, where five international players were among those to die, saw the game struggle even more from here on. The announcement that Argentina would be invited to form an expanded Four Nations competition and have their players join an extended Super 15 tournament, as long as they could meet certain conditions, represents an important development in the sport.

Although not having the traditions and history of the Five Nations championship, the Tri-Nations tournament developed rapidly into an important product. The associated development was arguably the key symbol of open professionalism for Murdoch's investment necessitated that the Super 12 (now soon to be Super 15) tournament was deliberately developed as a spectacle and a form of entertainment as something different from international test matches (Gilson et al., 2000). Quite what this will mean for Argentinean rugby remains to be seen and it is likely that a further repositioning will take place whereby they play more of their international rugby outside of Argentina. Important to note in discussions here is the relative power of different nations in the governance of the game, and issues closer to the shores of the leading southern hemisphere powers also need revisiting.

The case of the Pacific Islands also powerfully conveys some of the issues at the heart of rugby's struggles to develop. While many have pointed to the large number of Fijian, Samoan and Tongan players who have appeared for the national teams of Australia and New Zealand, it is also noted that these two nations need to visit the islands and play test matches there if they are to support the development of rugby in the region. Of course in aiding the strengthening of these teams this may also represent a real challenge to the hegemonic power and status of the big two so that from a playing perspective there are reasons why they would not want to see too much development. Bryan Williams, the former coach of the national team, suggested that if rugby was meant to be a big family then excluding Samoa from Super 12 competition and the poor treatment of his country was tantamount to child abuse (Richards, 2007). The big issue of course, as Richards (2007: p. 258) pointed out, was that 'Rupert Murdoch was never going to sell many satellite-television subscriptions to the impoverished folk of Apia, Suva or Nuku'alofa.' The Fiji coach Brad Johnstone made a similar observation when he noted that 'the Pacific nations' problem is that there aren't enough television sets and modern sport is promoted by bean-counting businessmen' (in Howitt and Haworth, 2002: p. 30). An even greater threat to the development of the international teams on the islands could be the increased movement of younger players to Japan where they can be tempted by university scholarships and posts with major corporations (Sakata, 2004).

The global, glocal and grobal

In the more general books on globalization sport is often excluded. Such an omission seems strange for few activities have the international reach of sport. Where sport is mentioned then it is rare that rugby union is ever part of any discussion where the focus remains largely on association football and/or the attempts to develop 'American' sports beyond national boundaries as part of a wider thesis on Americanization. Rugby's omission is not really that surprising given the game's failure to embrace much of the world. Rowe (2003) has suggested that sport is constitutively unsuited to the carriage of globalization in its fullest sense and that 'sport's compulsive attachment to the production of national difference may, instead, constitutively repudiate the embrace of the global' (p. 292). As Jackson and Andrews (1999) noted the local and the global can only be understood in relation to each other and that 'globalization itself is constituitive of, and constituted by, multiple processes which are engaged to differing degrees, at differing intensities, and in differing spatial locations' (p. 32). I hope that the examples used in this book have clearly shown this. Although such language has been criticized (Connell, 2007), scholars advocating discourses of glocalization and grobalization have attempted to tease out some of the central issues here in regard to local/global relations.

Glocalization, taken from the Japanese word *dochakuka*, which means global localization, highlights how global processes are always understood in a local context (Robertson, 1992, 1995). Here while a sport may be played globally it takes on different meanings and identities in particular places (Giulianotti and Robertson, 2009). Horton (2009) has applied this to explain the positioning of rugby union in Australia and concludes that 'although symbiotic relationships between local and global sport cultures exist, the impact of an individual cultural context is still the dominant influence in such relationships' (p. 980). This is an important point often overlooked in discussions of local/global relations for all interactions are contextually bound and need to be read within a particular social and cultural framework.

Grobalization focuses more on how large nations and powerful corporations are intent on imposing themselves upon various geographic areas. Here global processes overwhelm the local rather than integrate the two (Ritzer, 2007). Andrews and Ritzer (2007) have suggested that in the sports world, as in many other spheres, the local has been so affected by the global that it has become to all intents and purposes glocal (see also, Ritzer, 2007). Rowe's (2003: p. 281) comments concerning the 'mantra-like status of the concept of globalization' and the varying meanings of the term should also be acknowledged at this point in trying to better understand the interplay of relationships outlined above. In attempting to tie things together three key themes seem central to the current positioning and future development of the sport. I consider these to be the postmodernization, Olympianization and footballization of rugby union.

The postmodernization of rugby union

As noted in Chapter 1, while globalization itself is not as new as is often presented, the process has intensified during the postmodern period (Robinson, 2007). Applying this to the sport of rugby offers an interesting and pertinent time to assess just how the game has changed. What the professionalization and increased internationalization of rugby has led to is a suggested postmodernization of the sport. Given that amateurism had been built around modernity it seems apt to refer to the professionalization of the game since 1995 as the postmodern period for the sport (Skinner, Stewart and Edwards, 2003). If modernity is read as being about economic and social certitude and progress, then the postmodern encompasses negotiated or contested meaning and uncertainty (Rowe and Lawrence, 1996). Certainly the turbulent change towards the open professionalization of rugby has visibly highlighted the uncertainty. The preceding chapters have touched upon the continued debates over foreign imports, club versus country requirements and player eligibility that reflect contested meanings over local, regional and national aspirations. As indicated in the Introduction to this text the dramatic shift from amateurism to professionalism, coupled alongside the forces of globalization, meant that the sport changed very quickly and that these tensions often manifested themselves in a strong resistance to a perceived modernization of the game. Indeed, while I agree with Skinner, Stewart and Edwards (2003) that the game is undergoing a postmodernization, many of the ongoing tensions are a result of the sport struggling to adjust to aspects of modernity. I hope that I have managed to provide a balanced account that illustrates the interplay between different interests that has not 'decentred' the analysis too far away from the core and in the direction of the periphery (after Andrews and Ritzer, 2007) in describing these changes.

The initial professionalization of the game showed that despite its apparent inevitability few countries were really prepared for it. As Johnson (2000: p. 192) put it:

> In 1995 rugby made the final leap from the shrinking world of amateurism into full-blown professionalism and, as leaps go, it was every bit as astounding as the one made by Bob Beamon at the 1968 Olympics, when he almost cleared the long-jump pit, or Evel Knievel launching his motorbike over seventeen double-decker buses. Knievel ended up being extricated from a heap of twisted metal and loaded into the back of an ambulance, which is very nearly what happened to rugby as well.

Of course it was the formation of SANZAR that finally led to the open professionalization of the sport. Therefore it is no surprise that these three nations took to professionalism much easier than their foundation union cousins in the northern hemisphere. Off the field the transition was a much smoother one and on the field they have dominated much of the professional era to date. Yet the greater financial rewards now offered in England and France mean that the three leading southern hemisphere nations face a real struggle to keep their best players in the region. The decision to grant Daniel Carter a rugby 'sabbatical' may well be the first of many such arrangements in future years.

The Olympianization of rugby union

Another stated aim to develop the sport has been to get rugby (re)admitted into the Olympic Games. The sport had previously been played in the Olympics although last featured in 1924 when a team from the US took the gold medal providing a little-known answer to the quiz question, 'Who are the reigning Olympic rugby champions?' Even less well known is that they were one of only three teams to enter. That rugby was ever played in the Olympics owes much to Pierre de Coubertin who was a great advocate for the sport even though this is rarely mentioned in his biographies. Over a century on from its Olympic debut the President of the IOC, Jacques Rogge, announced that rugby would again be an Olympic sport in 2016. The fact that Rogge had himself played international rugby for Belgium must have certainly helped here. Steps in the right direction had already been made with the inclusion of Sevens in the 2002 Commonwealth Games in Manchester and its planned debut at the 2011 Pan American Games in Guadalajara.

The IOC were somewhat taken aback by the forcefulness of rugby's campaign to be part of the games. The promotional video cleverly included many images of women's rugby and a cast as diverse as possible to show that the sport was a global one. While rugby enthusiasts would recognize this as 'globaloney' (Veseth, 2005) the political game of inclusion was mastered well. In addition to Jonah Lomu, probably the most recognizable rugby player in the world but still not a global sporting figure (see Grainger, Newman and Andrews, 2005), the presentation team also featured Gus Pichot (Argentina) and IRB President Bernard Lapasset. The rest of the presenters would have been less known to much of the rugby fraternity as Kenya Sevens captain Humphrey Kayange joined forces with Australia's Cheryl Soon and Kazakhstan's Anastasia Knanova. Somewhat bizzarely, but as a reflection on the politics of inclusion, the revised and updated promotional video featured children running with a rugby ball through the streets somewhere in India. Of course this was not a real reflection of a world governed by a small power elite, and a sport played to a great extent in just a handful of nations, but was certainly par for the course at a time when buzzwords of inclusion and diversity loom large.

While many have been critical of the IRB in their failure to develop the game this campaign was a very clever one and rugby's Olympic status certainly promises much in developing the sport in certain nations. It is not known what this change will mean for the 'real' game of rugby, the fifteen-man sport that has been the focus of the present study. There will be clashes of dates, particularly for the southern hemisphere teams. The complex club versus country debate that has characterized the professional game in many of the home unions may also be affected. A British team will have to represent the Isles and as the whole history of the game is one of conflict between these nations this will be an interesting process to observe. Women may be included but there are few (if indeed any) examples of where male and female rugby players receive equal treatment and rewards. Rugby, in many ways, remains something of a male preserve (Sheard and Dunning, 1973) and an arena where dominant notions of hegemonic masculinity still remain omnipresent (Nauright and Chandler, 1996).

In identifying the significance of rugby's inclusion the IRB's Chief Executive Officer Mike Miller is worth quoting at some length:

I don't think people realise yet how big this could be for rugby. The Olympic Games is the biggest stage in the world for sport, we have currently 116 members, there are 205 nations involved in the Olympics, so right away you have to imagine that a number of those countries will say 'we want to join the rugby revolution, we want to set up a union', because they can see – particularly from the Rugby World Cup Sevens, all the upsets that took place and the first women's tournament – that there are medal opportunities and that's what countries want to see – the fact that they have a chance. So there would be a lot more interest from around the world and even more interest in the IRB Sevens World Series, it would be massive for the game. In countries like Russia, China, the USA – big markets – it would make a huge difference. For instance in Russia they are only allowed to have Olympic sports on the schools curriculum so at the moment rugby's growing there, they've got a pro league and they have it shown on television, but they have to have after-school clubs, which makes it that much harder. If we're in the Olympics it will be taught in schools, and that's the way you grow rugby. So yes, this could be a huge decision for rugby.

That it is the much shorter and easier to understand, seven-aside version of the sport included in 2016 makes sense given many of the issues I have outlined in this text. This may give more countries the chance to legitimately compete for medals but there are still many questions to be resolved about what this will really mean. If the best players are not made available for this then rugby could follow baseball and be excluded from the games in a short period of time. Another scenario is that Sevens could take over in popularity from the larger game. The condensed version of the game fulfills much of the criteria for both entertainment value and of course is a much easier activity to develop in a wider sphere. The recent performance of the Kenyan male team and the Ugandan women's team in major tournaments clearly conveys this. Small nations like Fiji are also much more competitive in Sevens. Part of the negotiation involved in gaining Olympic status was that it would be the premier event in the sport so the Rugby World Cup Sevens will cease to exist before 2016. If Sevens is to really take off then there could indeed be a sizeable power shift with a different group of nations dominating this version of the sport.

Rugby union is a complex game to understand with a myriad of rules and laws that many players themselves do not fully comprehend. Historically when its leading exponents from north and south have met there has been much contention and debate as to interpretation of these laws and the best way forward for the sport. The recent experimental law variations (ELV's) provoked much discussion and debate. The professionalization of rugby promised, among other things, financial riches and occurred alongside the increased commodification of association football. Few could fail to notice the remarkable transformation of football as it became a massive global business and for many provided the marker that rugby should aspire to. Before moving on to some concluding remarks I will consider whether we are witnessing a footballization of rugby and what this means.

The footballization of rugby

An increasingly common theme visible in a range of media sources, in parts of the northern hemisphere at least, is the comparison of rugby to football. I have used football as a reference point on numerous occasions throughout this work as the two are historically so entwined (Dunning, 1999). In identifying differences, as outlined in Chapter 4, much of this seems to be centered upon class-based ideologies. Football is positioned as being all about greed, corruption, cheating, and a sport that has sold its soul (Bower, 2003; Sugden and Tomlinson, 1998). Proponents of rugby have often taken this as being reflective of epitomizing everything rugby is not. Rugby is about honesty, virtue and character employing a language that still resonates with *Tom Brown's Schooldays* and discourses of muscular Christianity. Yet recent incidents involving players behaving badly off the field, the 'Bloodgate' scandal and the obvious manipulation of the rules to allow uncontested scrummages on the field, have challenged these ideals.

What much of the discussion really entails is a critique of commercialization. A win-at-all-costs mentality pervades within sports where the rewards become ever bigger. The case of Major League Baseball where the prevalence of performance-enhancing substances has markedly altered the positioning of the sport in the social and cultural landscape is an obvious example here. While there is no indication that rugby has followed this path the prevalence of shoulder injuries is the latest area for medical professionals within the game to address and various research has highlighted concerns about injury-rates as players become bigger (e.g. Bathgate et al., 2002; Brooks et al., 2005). Professionalism also saw the birth of players unions in many nations as the sport became the only form of employment for some men (Dabascheck, 2003).

Yet to disparage football is a dangerous strategy. Attempting to hold the moral high ground regarding greed and corruption is strange, for more than a century the sport of rugby union existed on a pretence of amateurism. To view 1995 as the start of professional rugby would in some respects be wrong, for amateurism was dead long before that. Jonathan Davies (1989) noted that he was a professional rugby player long before he moved to rugby league. Steve Black, the somewhat unorthodox but incredibly popular fitness and conditioning coach who has experience working with elite athletes in both sports, made a particularly illuminating point when observing the differences between football and rugby players:

> The latter are tougher, more intelligent and more capable of being empowered. However, there are signs that it might not stay that way as the money and high profile the new generation of

rugby players is receiving could have a negative effect on their attitude.

(Black, 2004: p. 112)

As the game becomes more commercialized, in some ways rugby players move closer to their football counterparts although of course they simultaneously continue to remain distant in commercial and economic terms. Those who become 'celebrities' face a different set of challenges and become key representatives of the sport in wider cultural contexts. Many of those who first invested in professional rugby in England did so because they saw the pound signs in football and thought that this could be replicated in rugby. They learned quickly that rugby was a different world and many exited from the sport with significant financial losses.

Concluding remarks: An odd-shaped world

RUGBY FOOTBALL: a game for hooligans played by gentlemen, for whom – until the ghastly advent of professionalism, beep [sic] tests, pasta diets and early nights – it was an exercise in identifying who could sing the dirtiest song after consuming a minimum twenty pints of ale, followed by a jolly amusing attempt to frighten the occupants of a family saloon with several hairy bottoms pressed up against the back window of the team coach on the way home.

(Johnson, 2000: p. 9)

In his essay on the early development of the rugby world cup Hutchins (1998) suggested that rugby offers fertile ground for further study as it moves away from a staunch amateur base to 'that of global corporate cultural capitalism' (p. 47). He suggests that this provides insight into 'the dominant practices within the continually emerging and developing global sporting political economy' (Hutchins, 1998: p. 47). Many other sports are now actively pursuing an internationalization or globalization agenda and even the most insular North American sports such as football, which of course originated from rugby, now aggressively pursues opportunities overseas. In (association) football Giulianotti and Robertson (2009) refer to an increased focus on the Asianization and Americanization of the game as guiding future developments in the sport. There seems little doubt that these will also form an integral part of the future of rugby as evidenced already by the decision to award the 2019 world cup finals to Japan. We can expect to see an even greater focus on developing the sport in the country although it may be more apt at this present time to refer instead to a 'Japanization' of rugby in tracking these changes. That Japan should be at the heart of this is important for rugby, as they are an economically powerful nation and a key player in wider globalization discourses. Also of interest here is the movement of migrant workers to Japan from the islands of the Pacific outside the core of the rugby world. Nico Besnier's ongoing research into the movement of Pacific Island rugby players to Japan will have much to contribute both in understanding hitherto neglected aspects of rugby union and athlete migration more generally.

As highlighted earlier Australia and New Zealand, when playing for the Bledisloe Cup in Hong Kong, took the game a step further along its internationalization agenda. Of course decisions such as this support the contention that globalization is effectively an expansion of commercialization and the motivation to take matches overseas is guided by a desire to tap into bigger and more lucrative markets. As Andrews and Grainger (2007: p. 486) note the unquestioned focus of sport 'is now on the production and delivery of entertaining mediated products and experiences designed to maximize profit'. The need to develop rugby in the US has already been discussed and will surely be an integral part of any future strategic initiatives to help the game grow.

There are many nations whom I have not mentioned much in this work. This as acknowledged from the outset reflects both the limitations of those governing rugby in developing the sport outside its core and my own linguistic limitations. Owing to my personal background and situatedness my work may also be viewed as adding to the 'northern theory of globalization' (Connell, 2007). Yet while this is not to deny a strong 'northern' focus to the study, rugby seems less open to such accusations given the prominence of three southern hemisphere nations in the rugby world. The plethora of research produced by sport scholars in New Zealand will also see to it that there is significant discussion of the globalization of rugby from a different vantage point.

It could be argued that in some ways professionalism has undermined the globalization of the sport. Smaller, and less wealthy, nations have had to play in world cup competitions and other tournaments without many of their best players. Rugby is a hard, physical game where a career-ending injury could be just one match away. The movement of players across borders and to different parts of the world offers up some interesting avenues for future work. In Japan, Light, Hirai and Ebishima (2008) have highlighted how the changes brought about by globalization and the professionalization of rugby have led to a decline in the game's popularity as many of the traditions have been eroded but have not been replaced by an exciting form of sport as entertainment.

A decade ago Hutchins and Phillips (1999: pp. 159–60) posed the question 'Can the world cup offer genuine opportunities to non-traditional rugby countries or will the game remain a celebration of former British colonies and their masculine prowess even if in commodified form?' The last ten years have shown that few other nations have been able to make their mark on the game's biggest stage. There is hope that the entry of rugby into the Olympic fold can aid in the game's development in peripheral nations although, as outlined above, the interrelationship between the two forms of the game has not been discussed in any detail. The IRB must be applauded for the monies invested in the game in Tier 2 nations since 2005, although again the importance of the world cup as the financial base of international development begs the question as to how New Zealand could have been awarded the 2011 tournament when staging it in Japan would surely have brought in significant profits.

Although the focus of this work has been centred on the professional game and the changes to rugby's international positioning since 1995, it is important to note that for the vast percentage of those who play and watch the sport the game remains decidedly amateur. Professional rugby is just the tip of the iceberg but increasingly appears to be morphing into something unrecognizable from the rest of the game. The greatest challenge seems to be retaining the very things that made rugby unique and special while facing the realities of commercial sport in a highly competitive market. Earlier on I noted the role of nostalgia in the game but there is a danger that we focus too much on this. As Smith (2008: p. 157) eloquently states:

We should not always blame professionalism, or over-romanticize an amateur idyll. Much of sport has got better – and long may it continue to do so. But we will miss some facets of the old world, even as it disappears.

In local–global relations it is important not to fall into another simplistic dichotomy that positions the pre-television game as reflecting all that is good and of cultural worth while the postmodern game signifies 'an inexorable slide into a rootless and corrosive entrepreneurial swamp' (J. Williams, 1994: p. 393).

Professional rugby is certainly a lot 'cleaner' than its amateur predecessor in terms of what happens on the field of play. With cameras able to look at incidents from every angle gratuitous violence is less of an issue than before. As Lewis and Winder (2007: p. 213) have noted 'rugby is a political, economic and cultural complex – more than a game, but also more than a business'. Concern over the 'Adidasification' of the All Blacks reflects many of the tensions here whereby commercial forces are often viewed as the antithesis to national pride and playing for the jersey (Hope, 2002; Jackson and Hokowhitu, 2002; Scherer and Jackson, 2008). National pride through rugby is particularly important for those nations like New Zealand and Wales who are very much minor players in wider discourses of globalization.

Augustin (1999) argues that there is no necessary contradiction between the construction of the 'global village' and the preservation of pockets of locally based identity and that these pockets may even be strengthened in some cases (see also, Tomlinson, 2007). Augustin (1999) also points to merging the two stages of rugby's evolution. The first, as I have discussed, links to local cultures, concrete exchange and community, or in Friedman's (2000) terms 'the olive tree'. The second, 'the lexus' of the open game, is constructed by global culture and characterized by television images and delocalized practices. Augustin (1999: p. 210) posits that

> there can be no doubt that the international commercial logic which is currently injecting money into rugby has interfered with established systems of management, thus calling into question the ability to transform of clubs and national federations alike. These bodies must be adapted and reconfigured – which in reality often means that they must be modernized – in order to be in a position to gain access, perhaps, to the stage of post-modernity.

Yet rather than writing of globalization the changes in rugby may be more reflective of internationalization. McGovern's (2002) work on migration pattern to the English football league was discussed in Chapter 5 and offers some useful pointers that can be adopted when looking at professional rugby. McGovern (2002) noted that while the market for professional footballers is becoming more international in nature this has largely developed along regional lines rather than global ones. The nationalities represented in the leading European rugby leagues clearly demonstrate this. In fact given that fewer nations play rugby, we are dealing with noticeably narrower regional lines than that identified in the research on professional football. Labour migration is socially embedded and powerfully conveys the fact that rugby has failed to develop much beyond its established core. The sport has not seen the same exponential growth as association football as a commercial activity and the game is less established in a global sense. Despite the great success of the Heineken Cup competition I have also avoided any reference to Euoropeanization. Teams from six nations enter this tournament and representatives from just three of these have ever won the trophy. It is clear that the game needs to expand much further for such language to be used.

For many years rugby was played as an eight man game where the most powerful rugby-playing nations operated as a tight(ish) forward unit and kept the ball to themselves. At times this was a rolling maul of seven as South Africa served time in the sin bin yet was readily welcomed back into the fold. They may have frequently disagreed on how to move forward but the one thing they collectively failed to do was spread the ball wide. In school rugby the bigger and stronger boys dominate. To refer back to the origins of the game in the public schools, 'football' served as an excuse for organized bullying. The littlest boy may stand on the outside, shivering on the wing, as he waits in hope of the ball reaching him before the match is over. In international rugby terms the small players are the nations who are close to, yet simultaneously far removed from, the ball.

Eight-man rugby was a defining feature of the Pontypool team I referred to earlier in this chapter and who were a dominant force in the game during the latter part of the amateur era. In the age of increased commercialization and commodification the need to entertain has become more and more important to developing rugby as a product. Here then there is a need to expand, to move beyond a tight forward-controlled eight-man game, to a much more expansive and entertaining fifteen-man spectacle. Indeed, the substitution law means that increasingly at the highest level it is more of a twenty-two–man game now as impact players come on to alter the course of the action. Entertainment is the key and increasing the number of spectators in the stadium, watching on television and across the continents is the target. It would be fantastic if we were to approach a world cup with 15 or more teams genuinely having a chance of competing for the title. Even if the IRB's (2004) stated aim of having eight unions capable of reaching the final in 2011 was met we would be seeing significant progress.

As I conclude this work there is much debate about the direction the game is moving in and the ways in which the sport needs to adapt in an increasingly competitive environment. Rugby is undoubtedly at a crossroad as it attempts to navigate its way between the competing traditions of the local and the necessities that embracing aspects of the global entail. Tactical stalemates with seemingly endless bouts of kicking are one of the most recent concerns but we must not forget that the legacy of Webb Ellis is that 'he picked up the ball and ran with it'.

References

Albrow, M. (1996) *The Global Age*. Cambridge: Polity.

Allison, L. (2001) *Amateurism in Sport: An Analysis and a Defence*. London: Frank Cass.

Allison, L. (2005) 'The Curious Role of the USA in World Sport', in *The Global Politics of Sport: The Role of Global Institutions in Sport*, L. Allison (ed.). London: Routledge.

Amis, J. and Cornwell, T. B. (2005) (eds) *Global Sport Sponsorship*. Oxford: Berg.

Anderson, B. (1983) *Imagined Communities: Reflections on the Origins and Spread of Nationalism*. London: Verso.

Andrews, D. (2001) (ed.) *Michael Jordan Inc.: Corporate Sport, Media Culture, and Late Modern America*. Albany, NY: State University of New York Press.

Andrews, D. (2004) 'Sport in the Late Capitalist Moment', in *The Commercialisation of Sport*, T. Slack (ed.). London: Routledge.

Andrews, D. and Grainger, A. (2007) 'Sport and Globalization', in *The Blackwell Companion to Globalization*, G. Ritzer (ed.). Oxford: Blackwell.

Andrews, D. and Jackson, S. (2001) (eds). *Sport Stars: The Cultural Politics of Sporting Celebrity*. London: Routledge.

Andrews, D. and Ritzer, G. (2007) 'The Grobal in the Sporting Glocal', *Global Networks*, 7, 135–53.

Appadurai, A. (1990) 'Disjuncture and Difference in the Global Cultural Economy', *Theory, Culture and Society*, 7, 295–310.

Appadurai, A. (1996) *Modernity at Large: Cultural Dimensions of Globalization*. Minneapolis: University of Minnesota Press.

Appelbaum, R. and Robinson, W. (2005) *Towards a Critical Globalization Studies*. London: Routledge.

Armstrong, G. and Giulianotti, R. (2001) (eds) *Fear and Loathing in World Football*. Oxford: Berg.

Augustin, J. P. (translated by P. Dine) (1999) 'From One Stage to Another: French Rugby Caught between Local and Global Cultures', *Journal of European Area Studies*, 7, 197–210.

Back, L. (1998) 'Local/Global', in *Core Sociological Dichotomies*, C. Jenks (ed.). London: Sage.

Bairner, A. (2001) *Sport, Nationalism and Globalization: European and North American Perspectives*. Albany, NY: SUNY Press.

Bairner, A. (2009) 'National Sports and National Landscapes: In Defence of Primordialism. *National Identities*, 11, 223–39.

Bale, J. (1991) *The Brawn Drain*. Chicago: University of Illinois Press.

Bale, J. (1994) *Landscapes of Modern Sport*. London: Leicester University Press.

Bale, J. (2003) *Sports Geography* (2nd edn). London: Routledge.

Bale, J. and Maguire, J. (1994) (eds) *The Global Sports Arena: Athletic Talent Migration in an Interdependent World*. London: Frank Cass.

Bateman, A. with Rees, P. (2001) *There and Back Again*. Edinburgh: Mainstream.

Bathgate, A., Best, J., Craig, G. and Jamieson, M. (2002) 'A Prospective Study of Injuries to Elite Australian Rugby Union Players', *British Journal of Sports Medicine*, 36, 265–9.

Beck, U. (2000) *What is Globalization?* Cambridge: Polity.

Black, D. and Nauright, J. (1998) *Rugby and the South African Nation*. Manchester: Manchester University Press.

Black, S. with McKenzie, A. (2004) *Blackie: The Steve Black Story*. Edinburgh: Mainstream.

Bodis, J.P. (1987) *Histoire Mondiale du Rugby*. Toulouse: Privat.

Bower, T. (2003) *Broken Dreams: Vanity, Greed and the Souring of British Football*. London: Simon & Schuster.

Boyle, R. and Haynes, R. (2000) *Power Play: Sport, the Media and Popular Culture*. Harlow: Longman.

Brawley, S. (2009) 'Your Shire, Your Sharks: The Cronulla-Sutherland Sharks and Delocalization v. Glocalization in Australian Rugby League', *International Journal of the History of Sport*, 26, 1697–715.

Brooks, J., Fuller, C., Kemp, S. and Reddin, D. (2005) 'Epidemiology of Rugby Injuries in English Professional Rugby Union: Part 1, Match Injuries', *British Journal of Sports Medicine*, 39, 757–66.

Burchill, J. (2001) *Burchill on Beckham*. London: Jonathan Cape.

Burdsey, D. (2007) *British Asians and Football: Culture, Identity, Exclusion*. London: Routledge.

Butler, E. (2001) *The Tangled Mane: The Lions Tour to Australia 2001*. London: Bloomsbury Publishing.

Cannadine, D. (2003) *In Churchill's Shadow: Confronting the Past in Modern Britain*. Oxford: Oxford University Press.

Carlin, J. (2008) *Playing the Enemy: Nelson Mandela and the Game that Made a Nation*. London: The Penguin Press.

Carling, W. and Heller, R. (1995) *The Way to Win: Strategies for Success in Business and Sports*. London: Little, Brown and Co.

Carrington, B. and McDonald, I. (2001) (eds) *'Race', Sport and British Society*. London: Routledge.

Carter, A. with Bishop, N. (2008) *Seeing Red: Twelve Tumultuous Years in Welsh Rugby*. Edinburgh: Mainstream.

Cashmore, E. (1982) *Black Sportsmen*. London: Routledge and Kegan Paul.

Cashmore, E. (2002) *Beckham*. Cambridge: Polity.

Cashmore, E. (2006) *Celebrity/Culture*. London: Routledge.

Cashmore, E. and Parker, A. (2003) '"One David Beckham …?": Celebrity, Masculinity and the Soccerati', *Sociology of Sport Journal*, 20, 214–32.

Catt, M. (2007) *Landing on My Feet: My Story*. London: Hodder & Stoughton Ltd.

Chandler, T. and Nauright, J. (1996) 'Conclusion', in *Making Men: Rugby and Masculine Identity*, J. Nauright and T. Chandler (eds). London: Frank Cass.

Chandler, T. and Nauright, J. (1999) (eds) *Making the Rugby World: Race, Gender, Commerce*. London: Frank Cass.

Chiba, N. and Jackson, S. (2006) 'Rugby Player Migration from New Zealand to Japan', *Football Studies*, 9, 67–78.

Clayton, B. and Harris, J. (2004) 'Footballers' Wives: The Role of the Soccer Player's Partner in the Construction of Idealised Masculinity', *Soccer and Society*, 5, 317–35.

Clayton, B. and Harris, J. (2009) 'Sport and Metrosexual Identity: Sports Media and Emergent Sexualities', in *Sport and Social Identities*, J. Harris and A. Parker (eds). Basingstoke: Palgrave Macmillan.

Collins, T. (1998) *Rugby's Great Split*. London: Frank Cass.

Collins, T. (2006) *Rugby League in Twentieth Century Britain*. London: Routledge.

Collins, T. (2009) *A Social History of English Rugby Union*. London: Routledge.

Colman, M. (1996) *Super League: The Inside Story*. Sydney: Ironbark.

Connell, R. (2007) 'The Northern Theory of Globalization', *Sociological Theory*, 25, 368–85.

Crolley, L. and Hand, D. (2002) *Football, Europe and the Press*. London: Frank Cass.

Dabascheck, B. (2003) 'Paying for Professionalism: Industrial Relations in Australian Rugby Union', *Sport Management Review*, 6, 105–25.

Dallaglio, L. (2007) *It's in the Blood: My Life*. London: Headline Publishing.

Daniell, J. (2009) *Confessions of a Rugby Mercenary*. London: Ebury Press.

Davies, J. with Corrigan, P. (1989) *Jonathan: An Autobiography*. London: Stanley Paul.

Delanty, G., Wodak, R. and Jones, P. (2008) (eds) *Identity, Belonging and Migration*. Liverpool: Liverpool University Press.

Dewey, R. (2008) 'Pacific Islands Rugby: Navigating the Professional Era', in *The Changing Face of Rugby: The Union Game and Professionalism since 1995*, G. Ryan (ed.). Newcastle: Cambridge Scholars Publishing.

Dine, P. (2001) *French Rugby Football: A Cultural History*. Oxford: Berg.

Dunning, E. (1999) *Sport Matters: Sociological Studies of Sport, Violence and Civilization*. London: Routledge.

Dunning, E. and Sheard, K. (1979) *Barbarians, Gentlemen and Players*. Oxford: Martin Robertson.

Dunning, E. and Sheard, K. (2005) *Barbarians, Gentlemen and Players* (2nd edn). London: Routledge.

Edensor, T. (2002) *National Identity, Popular Culture and Everyday Life*. Oxford: Berg.

Edwards, G. with Bills, P. (2003) *Tackling Rugby: The Changing World of Professional Rugby*. London: Headline.

Elliott, R. and Maguire, J. (2008) 'Thinking Outside of the Box: Exploring a Conceptual Synthesis for Research in the Area of Athletic Labour Migration'. *Sociology of Sport Journal*, 25, 482–97.

English, A. (2007) *Stand Up and Fight: When Munster Beat the All Blacks*. London: Yellow Jersey Press.

Falcous, M. and West, A. (2009) 'Press Narratives of Nation during the 2005 Lions Tour to Aotearoa-New Zealand', *Sport in Society*, 12, 156–73.

Farquharson, K and Majoribanks, T. (2003) 'Transforming the Springboks: Re-imagining the South African Nation through Sport', *Social Dynamics*, 29, 27–48.

Fitzsimons, P. (1996) *The Rugby War*. Sydney: HarperCollins.

Florida, R. (2008) *Who's Your City? How the Creative Economy is Making Where to Live the Most Important Decision of Your Life*. New York: Basic Books.

Friedman, T. (2000) *The Lexus and the Olive Tree: Understanding Globalization* (updated edn). New York: Anchor Books.

Friedman, T. (2007) *The World is Flat, 3.0*. New York: Picador.

Garland, I. (1993) *The History of the Welsh Cup, 1877–1993*. Wrexham: Bridge Books.

Garland, J. and Rowe, M. (1999) 'War Minus the Shooting? Jingoism, the English Press, and Euro 96', *Journal of Sport and Social Issues*, 23, 80–95.

Giles, D. (2000) *Illusions of Immortality: A Psychology of Fame and Celebrity*. Basingstoke: Palgrave Macmillan.

Gilson, C., Pratt, M., Roberts, K. and Weymes, E. (2000) *Peak Performance: Business Lessons from the World's Top Sports Organizations*. London: HarperCollins.

Giulianotti, R. (1999) *Football: A Sociology of the Global Game*. Cambridge: Polity.

Giulianotti, R. (2005) *Sport: A Critical Sociology*. Cambridge: Polity.

Giulianotti, R. and Robertson, R. (2007) 'Promoting the Social: Globalization, Football and Transnationalism', *Global Networks*, 7, 166–86.

Giulianotti, R. and Robertson, R. (2009) *Globalization and Football*. London: Sage.

Goldblatt, D. (2008) *The Ball is Round: A Global History of Soccer*. New York: Penguin.

Grainger, A. (2006) 'From Immigrant to Overstayer: Samoan Identity, Rugby, and Cultural Politics of Race and Nation in Aoteraroa/New Zealand, *Journal of Sport and Social Issues*, 30, 45–61.

Grainger, A. and Andrews, D. (2005) 'Resisting Rupert through Sporting Rituals? The Transnational Media Corporation and Global-Local Sport Cultures', *International Journal of Sport Management and Marketing*, 1, 3–16.

Grainger, A., Newman, J. and Andrews, D. (2005) 'Global Adidas: Sport, Celebrity and the Marketing of Difference', in *Global Sport Sponsorship*, J. Amis and T. B. Cornwell (eds). Oxford: Berg.

Green, M. and Oakley, B. (2001) 'Elite Sport Development Systems and Playing to Win: Uniformity and Diversity in International Approaches', *Leisure Studies*, 20, 247–67.

Greenwood, W. (2005) *Will: The Autobiography of Will Greenwood*. London: Arrow Books.

Grundlingh, A. (1995) 'The New Politics of Rugby', in *Beyond the Tryline: Rugby and South African Society*, A. Grundlingh, A. Odendaal and B. Spies (eds). Johannesburg: Ravan Press.

Hadley, I. (2001) *Codes of Misconduct: Birds, Booze and Brawls – My Life in International Rugby*. Bury: Milo Books.

Halberstam, D. (1999) *Playing for Keeps: Michael Jordan and the World He Made*. New York: Random House.

Hall, S. (1990) 'Cultural Identity and Diaspora', in *Identity: Community, Culture, Difference*, J. Rutherford (ed.). London: Lawrence and Wishart.

Hargreaves, J. (1994) *Sporting Females*. London: Routledge.

Harris, I. (2005) *There and Back Again: My Journey from League to Union and Back Again*. Edinburgh: Mainstream.

Harris, J. (1999) 'Lie Back and Think of England: The Women of Euro 96', *Journal of Sport and Social Issues*, 23, 96–110.

Harris, J. (2006) '(Re)presenting Wales: Celebrity and Identity in the Postmodern Rugby World', *North American Journal of Welsh Studies*, 6, 1–12.

Harris, J. (2007) 'Cool Cymru, Rugby Union and an Imagined Community', *International Journal of Sociology and Social Policy*, 27, 151–62.

Harris, J. (2008) 'Match Day in Cardiff: (Re)imaging and (Re)imagining the Nation', *Journal of Sport & Tourism*, 13, 297–313.

Harris, J. and Clayton, B. (2007) 'The First Metrosexual Rugby Star: Rugby Union, Masculinity and Celebrity in Contemporary Wales', *Sociology of Sport Journal*, 24, 145–64.

Harris, J. and Parker, A. (2009) (eds) *Sport and Social Identities*. Basingstoke: Palgrave Macmillan.

Hautboir, C. and Charrier, D. (2009) 'Local Economic and Social Impact of Multi-cities Mega-Sports Events: Case of the 2007 Rugby World Cup (RWC) in Paris Region', paper presented to the annual conference of the North American Society for Sport Management, Columbia, SC.

Healey, A. (2006) *Me and My Mouth: Austin Healey The Autobiography*. Wolvey: Monday Books.

Henson, G. with Thomas, G. (2005) *My Grand Slam Year*. Edinburgh: Mainstream.

Hickie, T. (1993) *They Ran with the Ball: How Rugby Football Began in Australia*. Melbourne: Longman Cheshire.

Higgs, R. (1995) *God in the Stadium: Sports and Religion in America*. Lexington: University of Kentucky Press.

Hill, R. with Lawrence, T. (2006) *Richard Hill: The Autobiography*. London: Orion.

Hobsbawm, E. (1991) *Nations and Nationalism Since 1780*. Cambridge: Cambridge University Press.

Hobsbawm, E. (2007) *Globalisation, Democracy and Terrorism*. London: Little, Brown.

Hoffman, S. (1992) *Sport and Religion*. Champaign, IL: Human Kinetics.

Holt, R. (1989) *Sport and the British*. Oxford: Oxford University Press.

Hope, W. (2002) 'Whose All Blacks?', *Media, Culture & Society*, 24, 235–53.

Horne, J. and Manzenreiter, W. (2006) 'An Introduction to the Sociology of Sports Mega-Events', in *Sports Mega-Events*, J. Horne and W. Manzenreiter (eds). New Jersey: Wiley.

Horsman, M. (1997) *Sky High: The Amazing Story of BSkyB – and the Egos, Deals ad Ambitions that Revolutionalised TV Broadcasting*. London: Orion.

Horton, E. (1995) *The Best World Cup Money Can Buy*. Oxford: Author.

Horton, P. (1996) '"Scapes" and "Phases": An Overview of Two Approaches to Sport and Globalization', *Social Forces*, 15, 6–10.

Horton, P. (2009) 'Rugby Union Football in Australian Society: An Unintended Consequence of Intended Actions', *Sport in Society*, 12, 976–85.

Houlihan, B. (1994) 'Homogenization, Americanization, and Creolization of Sport: Varieties of Globalization. *Sociology of Sport Journal*, 11, 356–75.

Howe, P.D. (1999) 'Professionalism, Commercialism and the Rugby Club: The Case of Pontypridd RFC', in *Making the Rugby World: Race, Gender, Commerce*, T. Chandler and J. Nauright (eds). London: Frank Cass.

Howe, P.D. (2001) 'An Ethnography of Pain and Injury in Professional Rugby Union: The Case of Pontypridd RFC', *International Review for the Sociology of Spurt*, 36, 289–303.

Howitt, B. and Haworth, D. (2002) *Rugby Nomads*. Auckland: HarperCollins.

Hutchins, B. (1996) 'Rugby Wars: The Changing Face of Football', *Sporting Traditions*, 13, 151–62.

Hutchins, B. (1998) 'Global Processes and the Rugby Union World Cup', *Football Studies*, 1, 34–54.

Hutchins, B. and Phillips, M. (1999) 'The Global Union: Globalization and the Rugby World Cup', in *Making the Rugby World: Race, Gender, Commerce*, T. Chandler and J. Nauright (eds). London: Frank Cass.

International Rugby Board (2004) *IRB Strategic Plan*. Dublin: IRB.

International Rugby Board (2008) *Playing Charter*. Dublin: IRB.

International Rugby Board (2009) IRB World Rankings (Accessed October, 2009).

Jackson, S. and Andrews, D. (1999) 'Between and Beyond the Global and the Local: American Popular Sporting Culture in New Zealand'. *International Review for the Sociology of Sport*, 34, 31–42.

Jackson, S., Batty, R. and Scherer, J. (2001) 'Transnational Sport Marketing at the Global/Local Nexus: The Adidasification of the New Zealand All Blacks', *International Journal of Sports Sponsorship and Marketing*, 3, 185–201.

Jackson, S. and Hokowhitu, B. (2002) 'Sport, Tribes and Technology: The New Zealand All Blacks Haka and the Politics of Identity', *Journal of Sport and Social Issues*, 26, 125–39.

Jameson, F. (1991) *Postmodernism, or, The Cultural Logic of Late Capitalism*. Durham, NC: Duke University Press.

Jarvie, G. and Walker, G. (1994) (eds) *Scottish Sport and the Making of the Nation: Ninety Minute Patriots?* Leicester: Leicester University Press.

Jenks, C. (1998) (ed.) *Core Sociological Dichotomies*. London: Sage.

Jennings, A. (1996) *The New Lords of the Rings: Olympic Corruption and How to Buy Gold Medals*. London: Pocket Books.

Jennings, A. (2006) *Foul! The Secret World of FIFA*. London: HarperCollins.

John, B. with Abbandonato, P. (2000) *Barry John: The King*. Edinburgh: Mainstream.

Johnes, M. (2005) *A History of Sport in Wales*. Cardiff: University of Wales Press.

Johnson, M. (2000) *Rugby and All That: An Irreverent History*. London: Hodder and Stoughton.

Jones, C. (2001) 'Mega-Events and Host-Region Impacts: Determining the True Worth of the 1999 Rugby World Cup', *International Journal of Tourism Research*, 3, 241–51.

Jones, S. (2000) *Midnight Rugby: Triumph and Shambles in the Professional Era*. London: Headline.

Kanter, R. (1977) *Men and Women of the Corporation*. New York: Basic Books.

Keating, F. (1993) *The Great Number Tens*. London: Partridge Press.

Kellner, D. (2002) 'Theorizing Globalization', *Sociological Theory*, 20, 285–305.

Kelly, S. (2008) 'Understanding the Role of the Football Manager in Britain and Ireland: A Weberian Approach', *European Sport Management Quarterly*, 8, 399–419.

Klein, A. (2006) *Growing the Game: The Globalization of Major League Baseball*. New Haven: Yale University Press.

Lanfranchi, P. and Taylor, M. (2001) *Moving with the Ball: The Migration of Professional Footballers*. Oxford: Berg.

Leonard, J. with Kervin, A. (2004) *Full Time: The Autobiography of a Rugby Legend*. London: HarperCollins.

Lewis, N. and Winder, G. (2007) 'Sporting Narratives and Globalization: Making Links between the All Blacks Tours of 1905 and 2005', *New Zealand Geographer*, 63, 202–15.

Light, R. (1999) 'Learning to be a 'rugger man': High School Rugby and Media Constructions of Masculinity in Japan', *Football Studies*, 2, 74–89.

Light, R. (2000) 'A Centenary of Rugby and Masculinity in Japanese Schools and Universities: Continuity and Change', *Sporting Traditions*, 16, 87–104.

Light, R., Hirai, H. and Ebishima, H. (2008) 'Tradition, Identity, Professionalism and Tensions in Japanese Rugby', in *The Changing Face of Rugby: The Union Game and Professionalism since 1995*, G. Ryan (ed.). Newcastle: Cambridge Scholars Publishing.

MacClancy, J. (1996) (Ed.) *Sport, Identity and Ethnicity*. Oxford: Berg.

Magee, J. (2006) 'Crossing the Gain Line? Welsh Rugby Union and South African Labour Migration', *Football Studies*, 9, 50–65.

Magee, J. and Sugden, J. (2002) 'The World at Their Feet: Professional Football and International Labour Migration', *Journal of Sport and Social Issues*, 26, 421–37.

Maguire, J. (1994) 'Sport, Identity Politics and Globalization: Diminishing Contrasts and Increasing Varieties', *Sociology of Sport Journal*, 11, 398–427.

Maguire, J. (1996) 'Blade Runners: Canadian Migrants and Global Ice-Hockey Trails', *Journal of Sport and Social Issues*, 20, 335–60.

Maguire, J. (1999) *Global Sport: Identities, Societies, Civilizations*. Cambridge: Polity.

Maguire, J. (2004) 'Sport Labor Migration Research Revisited', *Journal of Sport and Social Issues*, 28, 477–82.

Malcolm, D. (2006) 'Unprofessional Practice? The Status and Power of Sport Physicians', *Sociology of Sport Journal*, 23, 376–95.

Malcolm, D. and Sheard, K. (2002) 'Pain in the Assets: The Effects of Commercialization and Professionalization on the Management of Injury in English Rugby Union', *Sociology of Sport Journal*, 19, 149–69.

Malcolm, D, Sheard, K. and White, A. (2000) 'The Changing Structure and Culture of English Rugby Union Football', *Culture, Sport, Society*, 3, 63–87.

Malin, I. (1997) *Mud, Blood and Money: English Rugby Union Goes Professional*. Edinburgh: Mainsream.

Markovits, A. and Hellerman, S. (2001) *Offside: Soccer and American Exceptionalism*. Princeton: Princeton University Press.

McGovern, P. (2002) 'Globalization or Internationalization? Foreign Footballers in the English League, 1946–95', *Sociology*, 36, 23–42.

McRae, D. (2007) *Winter Colours: Changing Seasons in World Rugby* (3rd edn). Edinburgh: Mainstream.

Miller, T., Lawrence, G., McKay, J. and Rowe, D. (2001) *Globalization and Sport: Playing the World*. London: Sage.

Mills, C. W. (1959) *The Sociological Imagination*. New York: Oxford University Press.

Millward, P. (2006) 'We've All Got the Bug for Euro-Aways: What Fans Say about European Football Club Competition'. *International Review for the Sociology of Sport*, 41, 357–75.

Morton, A. (2000) *Posh & Becks*. London: Michael O'Mara Books.

Murray, B. (1998) *The World's Game: A History of Soccer*. Champaign, IL: University of Illinois Press.

Nash, C. and Collins, D. (2006) 'Tacit Knowledge in Expert Coaching: Science or Art?', *Quest*, 58, 465–77.

Nauright, J. (1994) 'Reclaiming Old and Forgotten Heroes: Nostalgia, Rugby and Identity in New Zealand', *Sporting Traditions*, 10, 131–9.

Nauright, J. and Chandler, T. (1996) (eds) *Making Men: Rugby and Masculine Identity*. London: Frank Cass.

Nicholls, T. (2006) *The Winter Game: Rediscovering the Passion of Rugby*. Edinburgh: Mainstream.

O'Brien, D. and Slack, T. (2004) 'Strategic Responses to Institutional Pressures for Commercialization: A case study of an English rugby union club', in *The Commercialisation of Sport*, T. Slack (ed.). London: Routledge.

Polley, M. (1998) *Moving the Goalposts: A History of Sport and Society since 1945*. London: Routledge.

Preuss, H. (2004) *The Economics of Staging the Olympics: A Comparison of the Games, 1972–2008*. Cheltenham: Edward Elgar.

Raney, A. and Bryant, J. (2006) (eds) *Handbook of Sports and Media*. Mahwah, NJ: Lawrence Erlbaum.

Redmond, S. and Holmes, S. (2007) (eds) *Stardom and Celebrity: A Reader*. London: Sage.

Richards, H. (2005) *Dragons and All Blacks: Wales and New Zealand, 1953 and a Century of Rivalry*. Edinburgh: Mainstream.

Richards, H. (2007) *A Game for Hooligans: The History of Rugby Union*. Edinburgh: Mainstream.

Ring, M. with Parfitt, D. (2006) *Ring Master: The Incredible Story of Welsh Rugby's Clown Prince*. Edinburgh: Mainstream.

Ritzer, G. (2007) *The Globalization of Nothing 2*. London: Pine Forge Press.

Roberts, K. (2004) *The Leisure Industries*. Basingstoke: Palgrave Macmillan.

Robertson, R. (1992) *Globalization: Social Theory and Global Culture*. London: Sage.

Robertson, R. (1995) 'Glocalization: Time-Space and Homogeneity-Heterogeneity', in *Global Modernities*, M. Featherstone, S. Lash and R. Robertson (eds). London: Sage.

Robins, K. (1991) 'Tradition and Translation: National Culture in a Global Context', in *Enterprise and Heritage*, J. Corner and S. Harvey (eds). London: Routledge.

Robinson, W. (2007) 'Theories of Globalization', in *The Blackwell Companion to Globalization*, G. Ritzer (ed.). Oxford: Blackwell.

Roche, M. (2000) *Mega-Events and Modernity: Olympics and Expos in the Growth of Global Culture*. London: Routledge.

Rojek, C. (2001) *Celebrity*. London: Reaktion Books.

Rojek, C. (2007) *Brit-myth: Who Do the British Think They Are?* London: Reaktion Books.

Rowe, D. (1995) *Popular Cultures: Rock Music, Sport, and the Politics of Pleasure*. London: Sage.

Rowe, D. (2003) 'Sport and the Repudiation of the Global', *International Review for the Sociology of Sport*, 38, 281–94.

Rowe, D. and Lawrence, G. (1996) 'Beyond National Sport: Sociology, History and Postmodernity', *Sporting Traditions*, 12, 3–16.

Ryan, G. (1993) *Forerunners of the All Blacks: The 1888–9 New Zealand Native Football Team in Britain, Australia and New Zealand*. Christchurch: Canterbury University Press.

Ryan, G. (2008) (ed.) *The Changing Face of Rugby: The Union Game and Professionalism since 1995*. Newcastle: Cambridge Scholars Publishing.

Sakata, H. (2004) The Influence of Foreign Players on the Transformation of Japanese Rugby over the Last Three Decades, unpublished MA thesis, University of Canterbury.

Scherer, J. and Jackson, S. (2008) 'Cultural Studies and the Circuit of Culture: Advertising, Promotional Culture and the New Zealand All Blacks', *Cultural Studies – Critical Methodologies*, 8, 507–26.

Scholte, J. (2000) *Globalization: A Critical Introduction*. Basingstoke: Palgrave Macmillan.

Sheard, K. and Dunning, E. (1973) 'The Rugby Football Club as a Type of Male Preserve: Some Sociological Notes', *International Review of Sport Sociology*, 5, 5–21.

Skinner, J., Stewart, B. and Edwards, A. (2003) 'The Postmodernisation of Rugby Union in Australia', *Football Studies*, 6, 51–69.

Slack, T. (2004) (ed.) *The Commercialisation of Sport*. London: Routledge.

Smart, B. (2005) *The Sport Star*. London: Sage.

Smith, A. (1999) 'An Oval Ball and a Broken City: Coventry, Its People and Its Rugby Team, Part 2, 1995–98', *International Journal of the History of Sport*, 16, 155–68.

Smith, A. (2000) 'Civil War in England: The Clubs, the RFU, and the Impact of Professionalism on Rugby Union, 1995–99', in *Amateurs and Professionals in Post-war British Sport*, A. Smith and D. Porter (eds). London: Frank Cass.

Smith, A. and Porter, D. (2000) (eds) *Amateurs and Professionals in Post-war British Sport*. London: Frank Cass.

Smith, D. and Williams, G. (1980) *Fields of Praise: The Official History of the Welsh Rugby Union, 1881–1981*. Cardiff: University of Wales Press.

Smith, E. (2008) *What Sport Tells us About Life*. London: Penguin Books.

Smith, S. (1999) *The Union Game: A Rugby History*. London: BBC Books.

Spectrum Value Partners and Addleshaw Goddard (2008) *Putting Rugby First: An Independent Report into Rugby's Global Future*. London: Spectrum Value Partners and Addleshaw Goddard.

Stewart, B., Nicholson, M., Smith, A. and Westerbeek, H. (2004) *Australian Sport: Better by Design? The Evolution of Australian Sport Policy*. London: Routledge.

Sugden, J. and Bairner, A. (1993) *Sport, Sectarianism, and Society in a Divided Ireland*. Leicester: Leicester University Press.

Sugden, J. and Tomlinson, A. (1998) *FIFA and the Contest for World Football: Who Rules the People's Game?* Cambridge: Polity.

Teaiwa, T. and Mallon, S. (2005) 'Ambivalent Kinship? Pacific People in New Zealand', in *New Zealand Identities: Departures and Destinations*, J. Liu, T. McCreanor, T. McIntosh and T Teaiwa (eds). Wellington: Victoria University Press.

Telfer, J. with Ferguson, D. (2005) *Looking Back ... For Once*. Edinburgh: Mainstream.

Thomas, C. (updated by G. Thomas) (2005) *The History of the British and Irish Lions*. Edinburgh: Mainstream.

Thomas, G. with Parfitt, D. (2007) *Alfie! The Gareth Thomas Story*. Edinburgh: Mainstream.

Ticher, M. (1994) 'Notional Englishmen, Black Irishmen and Multicultural Australians: Ambiguities in National Sporting Identity', *Sporting Traditions*, 11, 75–91.

Tomlinson, J. (1999) *Globalization and Culture*. Cambridge: Polity.

Tomlinson, J. (2007) 'Cultural Globalization', in *The Blackwell Companion to Globalization*, G. Ritzer (ed.). Oxford: Blackwell.

Tuck, J. (1996) 'Patriots, Barbarians, Gentleman and Players: Rugby Union and National Identity in Britain since 1945', *Sporting Heritage*, 2, 25–36.

Tuck, J. (2003) 'Making Sense of Emerald Commotion: Rugby Union, National Identity and Ireland', *Identities: Global Studies in Culture and Power*, 10, 495–515.

Tuck, J. and Maguire, J. (1999) 'Making Sense of Global Patriot Games: Rugby Players' Perceptions of National Identity Politics', *Football Studies*, 2, 26–54.

Turner, G. (2004) *Understanding Celebrity*. London: Sage.

Van Bottenburg, M. (translated by B. Jackson) (2001) *Global Games*. Urbana, IL: University of Illinois Press.

Veseth, M. (2005) *Globaloney: Unravelling the Myths of Globalization*. Lanham, MD: Rowman & Littlefield.

Wagg, S. (1984) *The Football World: A Contemporary Social History*. Brighton: Harvester Press.

Wagg, S. (1995) (ed.) *Giving the Game Away: Football, Politics, and Culture on Five Continents*. London: Leicester University Press.

Wagg, S. (2004) (ed.) *British Football and Social Exclusion*. London: Routledge.

Wagg, S. (2005) (ed.) *Cricket and National Identity in the Postcolonial Age*. London: Routledge.

Wagg, S. (2007) 'Angels of Us All? Football Management, Globalization and the Politics of Celebrity', *Soccer & Society*, 8, 440–58.

Wallerstein, I. (1974) *The Modern World System, Volume 1*. New York: Academic Press.

Wedderburn, M. (1989) 'You're Black, You're Quick, You're on the Wing: A Sociological Analysis of England's Elite, Black, Rugby Union Players', unpublished MSc thesis, University of Loughborough.

Weed, M. (2001) 'In-ger-land at Euro 2000: How Handbags at Twenty Paces was Portrayed as a Full-Scale Riot', *International Review for the Sociology of Sport*, 36, 407–24.

Weight, R. (2002) *Patriots: National Identity in Britain 1940–2000*. London: Pan Books.

Whannel, G. (2002) *Media Sport Stars: Masculinities and Moralities*. London: Routledge.

White, J. with Ray, C. (2007) *In Black and White: The Jake White Story*. Cape Town: Zebra Press.

Williams, G. (1991) *1905 and All That*. Llandysul: Gomer Press.

Williams, G. (1994) 'The Road to Wigan Pier Revisited: The Migration of Welsh Rugby Talent since 1918', in *The Global Sports Arena: Athletic Talent Migration in an Interdependent World*, J. Bale and J. Maguire (eds). London: Frank Cass.

Williams, G., Lush, P., Hinchliffe, D. and McCarthy, S. (2005) *Rugby's Berlin Wall: League and Union from 1895 to Today*. London: London League Publications.

Williams, I. (1991) *In Touch: Rugby – Life Worth Living*. London: Kingswood Press.

Williams, J. (1994) 'The Local and the Global in English Soccer and the Rise of Satellite Television', *Sociology of Sport Journal*, 11, 376–97.

Williams, J. and Wagg, S. (1991) (eds) *British Football and Social Change: Getting into Europe*. London: Leicester University Press.

Williams, M. with Thomas, S. (2009) *The Magnificent Seven: The Autobiography*. London: John Blake Publishing.

Williams, R. (1977) *Marxism and Literature*. Oxford: Oxford University Press.

Williams, R. (2004) 'The Experiences of Tongan Rugby Players in Wales', unpublished BSc dissertation, University of Wales.

Woodman, L. (1993) 'Coaching: A Science, An Art, An Emerging Profession', *Sport Science Review*, 2, 1–13.

Woodward, C. with Potanin, F. (2004) *Winning! The Story of England's Rise to Rugby World Cup Glory*. London: Hodder and Stoughton.

Wyatt, D. (1996) *Rugby Disunion: The Making of Three World Cups*. London: Victor Gollancz.

Index